拔尖创新人才英语系列教材
EFL Learning Series for Top-notch Innovative Talents
教育部人文社会科学研究一般项目(20YJC740106)

情境口语
Situational Oral English

主　编　周小兰
副主编　田庆强　左　宁　陈登峰
　　　　张维娜　李　红

山东大学出版社
SHANDONG UNIVERSITY PRESS
·济南·

图书在版编目(CIP)数据

情境口语:英文/周小兰主编.—济南:
山东大学出版社,2020.8(2022.9 重印)
ISBN 978-7-5607-6686-7

Ⅰ.①情… Ⅱ.①周… Ⅲ.①英语—口语
Ⅳ.①H319.9

中国版本图书馆 CIP 数据核字(2020)第 161733 号

责任编辑 张申华
封面设计 牛 钧

出版发行 山东大学出版社
社 址 山东省济南市山大南路 20 号
邮政编码 250100
发行热线 (0531)88363008
经 销 新华书店
印 刷 济南新科印务有限公司
规 格 787 毫米×1092 毫米 1/16
11.5 印张 341 千字
版 次 2020 年 8 月第 1 版
印 次 2022 年 9 月第 2 次印刷
定 价 48.00 元

Contents

Unit 1 International Flight

Part A Before Boarding

A1. Introduction

Tips for Attention Before Check-in

The basic structure of an international flight check-in works the same as a domestic flight: You present yourself and any luggage, along with your ID and boarding pass, and go through a few security checkpoints on your way to the plane. But there are a few key differences you should be aware of: You'll need to show up a little earlier; a passport is the only valid identification for international flights; for some countries you might need a visa; and on some U. S. -bound international flights, you'll clear customs and immigration before getting on the plane instead of after arriving at your destination.

When to arrive at the airport

As a general rule, most airlines recommend arriving at the airport at least two hours before departure for domestic flights and at least three hours before departure for international flights. And, for domestic flights, you should add a little extra time if you're traveling during peak periods when lines for security and at the ticket counter are likely to be long.

When you're calculating how early to get in that security line, it helps to know a few standard benchmarks. Although there's a lot of variance because of individual airport policies and screening policies for certain destinations, as a general rule, you'll be safe if you are checked in (along with any checked baggage) at least 90 minutes before your flight, and if you're at the gate, ready to board, by 45 to 60 minutes before departure time.

Tips

Always check with your airline before planning your timing for arrival at the airport. Airlines may impose special check-in requirements to specific international destinations, requiring you to check in several hours in advance and be at the boarding gate earlier than usual. There are a few particularly unusual cases, too. For example, if you're flying direct from Los Angeles to Cuba, you won't check in at the international terminal, and you'll need to pay for a Cuban tourist card — basically, a low-key visa — at the departure gate.

Documentation required for international travel

If you're traveling to or from the United States by air, you need a valid passport to board your plane and enter the destination country. But it's not enough for your passport to be valid at the time of entry; many countries require that your passport be valid for 30 days — or longer — past the planned end of your trip. Even if you're travelling to a country that doesn't impose this requirement, it's still a good idea, because it ensures that you'll have legal identification even if you become embroiled in a rare, but serious, travel snafu.

(Adapted from *traveltips. usatoday. com*)

A2. Words and Expressions

Vocabulary

1. domestic /də'mestɪk/ *adj.* 国内的
2. slack /slæk/ *adj.* 不紧的，松的
3. peak /piːk/ *n.* 最高点，高峰
4. boom /buːm/ *n.* 繁荣，增长
5. reservation /ˌrezər'veɪʃn/ *n.* 预定，预约
6. mash /mæʃ/ *v.* 捣成泥状（食）
7. standby /'stændbaɪ/ *n.* 备用，随时准备
8. upgrade /ˌʌp'greɪd/ *v.* 升级
9. overbook /ˌoʊvər'bʊk/ *v.* 超额订出，超额预订
10. compartment /kəm'pɑːrtmənt/ *n.* 舱，隔间，隔室

Book and Confirm Air Tickets	**预定和确定机票**
international flight	国际航班
domestic flight	国内航班

terminal	航站楼
slack / dull / off / low / dead season	淡季
peak period / boom season / busy season	旺季
first class	一等舱
business class	商务舱
economy class	经济舱
one-way ticket	单程票
return ticket	返程票
round-trip ticket	往返票
food reservation for kids below 2	预定童餐(不满两岁)
mashed fruit	水果泥
standby ticket	余票
fly standby	随时待飞
missed flight	错过的航班
early arrival	提前抵达
upgrade flight seat	升级座位舱
overbooked flight compartment	超额订出的机舱

Vocabulary

1. trolley /ˈtrɑːli/ *n.* 手推车
2. queue /kjuː/ *v.* 排队
3. agent /ˈeɪdʒənt/ *n.* 代理人
4. weigh /weɪ/ *v.* 称重
5. excess /ˈekses/ *n.* 过量
6. carrier /ˈkæriər/ *n.* 运输工具
7. aerodrome /ˈerədroʊm/ *n.* 飞机场

Check in	**办理登机手续**
put on the trolley	将(行李)放在推车上
queue up / line up	排队
ticket counter	取票前台
ticket agent	柜台员
flight ticket	机票
weigh your luggage on a (luggage) scale	行李称重
charge for your excess luggage	超重费

pay a fee	付费
stick a tag on	贴行李签
check-in luggage / checked luggage	托运行李
check in one's luggage	办理托运
carry-on bag / hand luggage	随身携带行李
backpack	背包

Flight Delays of Civil Planes	**航班延误**
arrival and departure monitor	班机抵达/出发时间显示屏
FLT NO. = flight number	航班号
departure	出发地
departure to	目的地
departure time	起飞时间
delayed	延误
boarding	正在登机
carrier operation and management	航空公司运行管理
air traffic control	流量控制
bad weather	恶劣天气
aerodrome aid	机场保障
unexpected circumstances	突发状况

Vocabulary

1. prohibit /prəˈhɪbɪt/ *v.* 禁止
2. sniffer /ˈsnɪfər/ *n.* 吸毒者
3. unbuckle /ʌnˈbʌkəl/ *v.* 解开
4. conveyor /kənˈveɪər/ *n.* 传送带
5. board /bɔːrd/ *v.* 上(飞机,火车,船)
6. wifi /ˈwaɪfaɪ/ *n.* 无线网
7. pass /pæs/ *n.* 通行证

Security Check	**安检**
security officer	安检人员
metal detector	金属探测器
prohibited items	违禁物品
remove liquid	清除液体携带物

sniffer dog	嗅探犬
X-ray machine	X 射线机
take off your shoes	脱鞋
empty your pockets	清空口袋
unbuckle your belt	解下皮带
put your bag on the conveyor belt	将包放上传送带
put electronic appliance in a tray	将电子产品放入托盘
walk through the metal detector	通过安检门

The Gate	**登机口**
boarding / waiting area	登机/等待区
departure lounge	候机大厅
free wifi	免费无线网
check-in counter	登机办理前台
check in at the gate	办理登机
get your boarding pass	拿登机牌
board the plane	登机

A3. Situational Conversations

Conversation 1 At the Check-in Desk

Dan is flying from New York to Los Angeles. When he arrives at the airport, he goes to the check-in desk. Listen to the conversation between Dan and the agent:

A: Agent **D**: Dan

A: Good afternoon! **Where are you flying to today**?

D: Los Angeles.

A: May I have your passport, please?

D: **Here you go.**

A: Are you **checking any bags**?

D: Just this one.

A: OK, please place your bag on the **scale.**

D: I have a **stopover** in Chicago. Do I need to pick up my luggage there?

A: No, it'll **go straight through** to Los Angeles. Here are your **boarding passes.** Your flight leaves from gate 15A and it'll **begin boarding** at 3:20. Your seat number is 26E.

D: Thanks.

(Adapted from *espressoenglish. net*)

☞**Notes**

- **"Where are you flying today?"**: Instead of this, the agent may ask "What's your final destination?" The answer will be the same!
- **"Here you go."**: You can say it anytime you give something to somebody.
- **check your bags**: It means to put them on the airplane inside the cargo compartment. The small bag you take with you on the airplane is called a carry-on. You need to put your carry-on bags through the X-ray machine at security.
- **scale**: It is the equipment that tells you the weight of your luggage (45 kilograms, for example).
- **stopover or layover**: It means when the airplane stops in a different city before continuing to the final destination.
- **go straight through**: It means your luggage will go directly to the final destination (and you don't need to pick it up during your stopover).
- **boarding passes**: They are the tickets that permit you to enter the airplane.
- **begin boarding**: It means that the passengers start to enter the plane. Typical boarding time is 30-60 minutes before takeoff.

⇨**Answer YES!**

- Did you pack your bags yourself?
- Has your luggage been in your possession at all times?
- Are you aware of the regulations regarding liquids in your carry-on?

⇨**Answer NO!**

- Are you carrying any firearms or flammable materials?
- Have you left your luggage unattended at any time?
- Has anyone given you anything to carry on the flight?

Conversation 2 Going through Security

A: Agent D: Dan

A: Please lay your bags flat on the conveyor belt, and use the bins for small objects.

D: Do I need to take my laptop out of the bag?

A: Yes, you do. Take off your hat and your shoes, too.

(He walks through the metal detector, and the alarm ***went off****.)*

[BEEP BEEPBEEP BEEP]

A: Please step back. Do you have anything in your pockets — keys, cell phone, loose change?

D: I don't think so. Let me try taking off my belt.

A: OK, come on through.

(*He goes through the metal detector again.*)

A: You're all set! Have a nice flight.

(Adapted from *espressoenglish.net*)

☞**Notes**

- **go through security:** There are two pieces of equipment in security. You put your bags through the X-ray machine, and you walk through the metal detector. Some airports also use a body scanner for a more careful check. The X-ray machine has a conveyor belt that moves your bags automatically through the machine. You can put small items like keys or money into plastic bins.
- **go off:** When the alarm sounds, we say "the alarm went off." To describe what caused the alarm to sound, we say "set off" — for example, "My keys set off the alarm" or "My keys set off the metal detector."
- **"You're all set!":** It is a common expression that means "you're finished and everything is OK."

Announcements at the Gate

Airports are divided into **terminals** (the major sections of the airport) and each terminal has many **gates**. The **gate** is the door you go through to enter the airplane. Here are a few announcements you might hear while you are at the gate, waiting for the plane to board.

1. "There has been a gate change."
   (It means the flight will leave from a different gate.)
2. "United Airlines flight 123 to New York is now boarding."
   (It means it's time for passengers to enter the plane.)
3. "Please have your boarding pass and identification ready for boarding."
4. "We would like to invite our first- and business-class passengers to board."
5. "We are now inviting passengers with small children and any passengers requiring special assistance to begin boarding."
6. "We would now like to invite all passengers to board."
   (It means everyone can enter the plane.)
7. "This is the final boarding call for United Airlines flight 123 to New York."
   (It means it is the final opportunity to enter the plane before they close the doors.)
8. "Passenger John Smith, please proceed to the United Airlines desk at gate 12."

   (Adapted from *espressoenglish.net*)

A4. Picture Knowledge

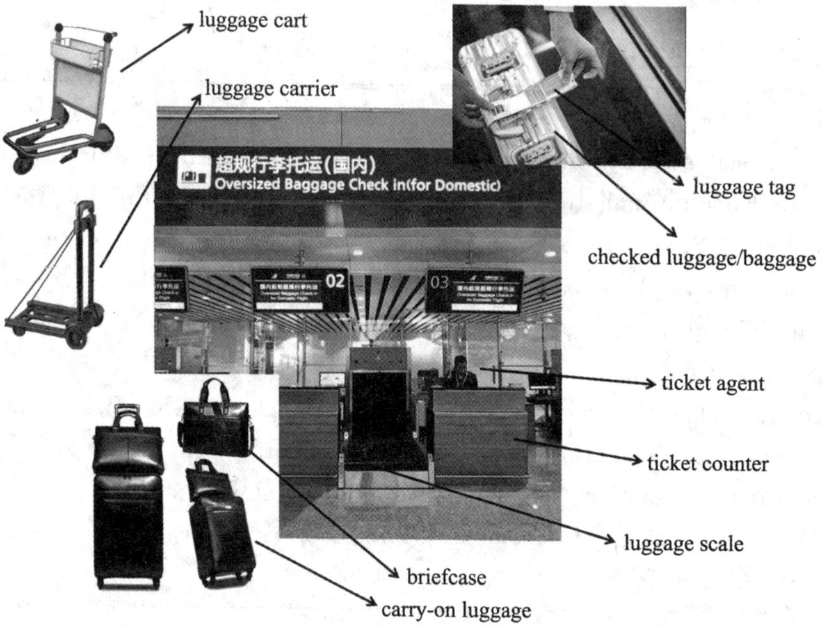

Pic. 1-1

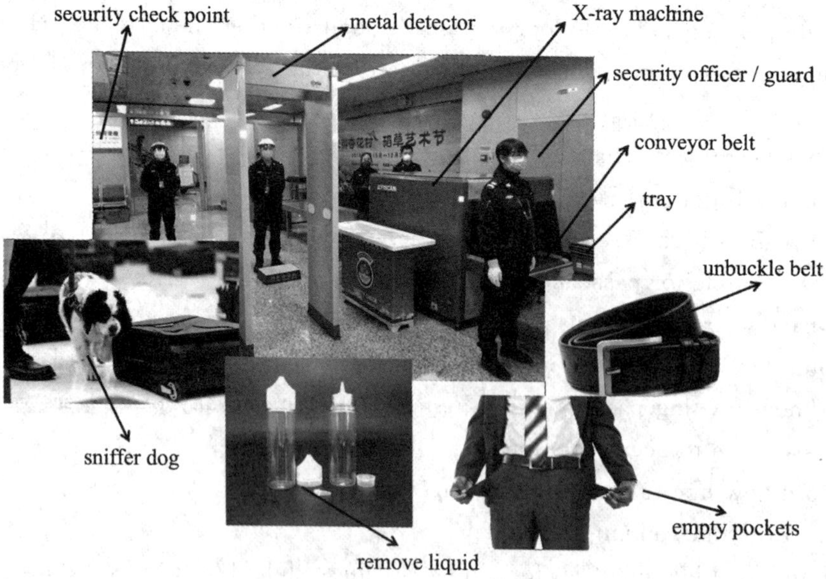

Pic. 1-2

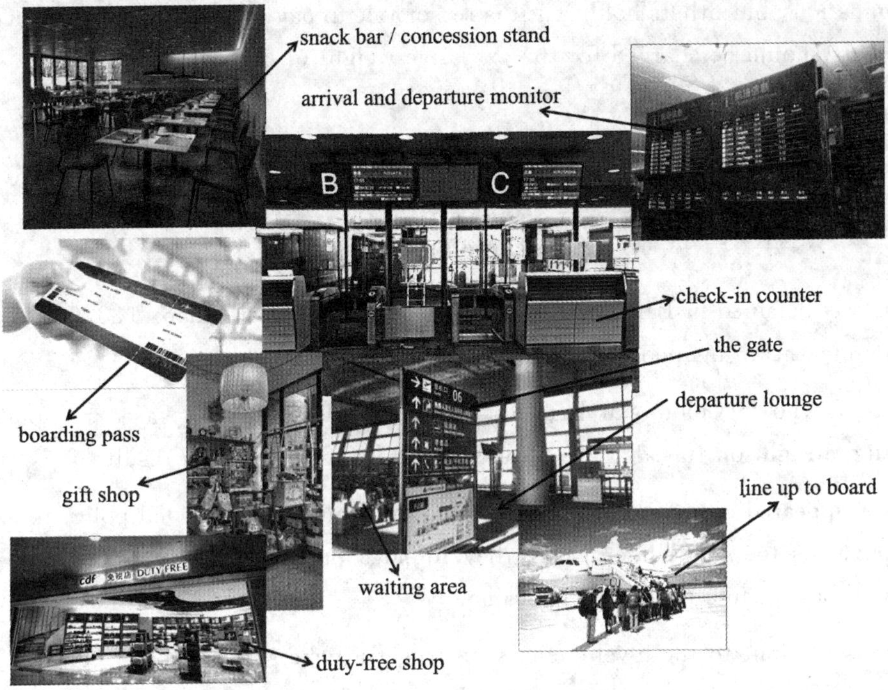

Pic. 1-3

A5. Speaking Activities

Role Play

Design a conversation between a ticket agent and a passenger for checking in, your conversation should cover the procedures for getting the ticket, checking luggage in, the fee for excess luggage weight, reminder for the liquid rule on carry-on bags.

You may refer to the expressions below but don't confine yourself to them.

Suggested Expressions:

Your passport and your e-ticket (paper-ticket), please!
How many pieces of baggage / luggage do you have?
I have a huge suitcase, a carry-on bag and a backpack.
Are you checking the backpack or carrying on?
Sorry, your luggage is 2 kilos overweight!
How much is the excess baggage charge?

Discussion

Conduct a pair discussion and summarize your viewpoints on the topic: ***Is it proper to charge the obese passengers for extra fee?*** Some argue that it is an utter discrimination, but others hold that it is reasonable to pay for extra occupied space since passengers should be charged for the excessive weight of luggage.

Retelling

Read the story below and retell it to the class with details.

Cocaine Smuggling

A man was detained in Barcelona for trying to smuggle more than $33,000 worth of cocaine underneath his poorly fitted wig, police said.

The man, who is Colombian but has yet to be identified, appeared nervous when departing a flight on June 18. He drew suspicion from police as a result.

His hair appeared dramatically outsized, reported Reuters, which led police to ask him to remove his toupee. Underneath, they found a package filled with more than 500 grams — more than a pound — of cocaine.

"There is no limit to the inventiveness of drug traffickers," Barcelona police said in a statement Tuesday, according to Reuters.

An undated handout composite photo released by the Spanish National Police on 16 July, 2019 shows a man who was detained at Barcelona's El Prat airport allegedly carrying 500 grams cocaine hidden under a wig.

Police released two mugshots of the man, one in which he's still wearing the toupee and the other showing the package of cocaine on his head. His eyes are concealed in both images.

It is unclear whether the man, who was charged with a public health violation, was still being detained.

(Adapted from *usatoday. com*)

Interpretation

Interpret the following paragraphs into English with what you have learned in Part A.

Paragraph 1

由于忘记带护照,再加上交通堵塞,John到达机场的时候,飞机已经起飞了。于是,他只能更换机票等待下一个航班。因为处在旺季,John排了好久的队才顺利通过安检门到达候机大厅。为了避免再次误机,他时刻关注显示屏直到成功登机。当飞机在芝加哥临时停留时,John在免税店为家人购置了礼物。经过长达十几个小时的旅程,他终于抵达家乡。

Paragraph 2

Peter 一到机场，就立刻赶到前台办理登机手续。他将旅行箱办理了托运，付完超重费后，领取了登机牌。然后，他前往安检处，在工作人员的示意下，将随身携带的背包及物品放到了传送带上。但在他走过安检门时，警报响起，于是他不得不接受嗅探犬的搜查，这导致他错过了航班。值得庆幸的是，他成功申请了待飞，并且免费升级了座位，最终登上前往纽约的航班。

Paragraph 3

今天我从北京去伦敦出差。北京真冷啊，我感觉被冻得手脚发麻。现在是淡季，旅客不多，机票很好预定。我提前抵达航站楼，将行李放在推车上，排队安检。我只去三天，因此我只有随身携带的行李，不需要办理托运。安检人员用 X 射线机检查是否有违禁物品，同时让我清空口袋并脱鞋。结果发现，我包内有一支大容量牙膏，不能带上飞机。由于恶劣天气突发，航班延误了两个小时才起飞。真是糟透的一天！

A6. Extension

Synonym Discrimination

Can you figure out the differences among the words below?

Group 1: trip / journey / tour / guide / voyage / excursion / expedition
Group 2: book / reserve

Extensive Reading

Security Administration for Liquid

Passengers are allowed to bring a quart-sized bag of liquids, aerosols, gels, creams and pastes in your carry-on bag and through the checkpoint. These are limited to travel-sized containers that are 3.4 ounces (100 milliliters) or less per item. Placing these items in the small bag and separating from your carry-on baggage facilitates the screening process. Pack items that are in containers larger than 3.4 ounces or 100 milliliters in checked baggage.

Any liquid, aerosol, gel, cream or paste that alarms during screening will require additional screening.

Exemptions

- Medications

You are allowed to carry as much liquid medicine as required for your trip, even if this exceeds the usual limit on liquids, provided you have a supporting prescription or doctor's note. The medicine does not need to fit in the transparent bag but you should have it ready for inspection by airport security.

- Infant and child nourishments

If you are travelling with a baby or infant you are allowed to carry as much baby milk, powdered formula, sterilized water (must be in a baby bottle) and baby food as required for your trip, even if this exceeds the usual limit on liquids. These do not need to fit in the transparent bag but you should have them ready for inspection by airport security.

- Inbound International Flights

You may carry duty free liquids in secure, tamper-evident bags, more than 3.4 oz or 100 ml in your carry-on bag if: The duty free liquids were purchased internationally and you are traveling to the United States with a connecting flight.

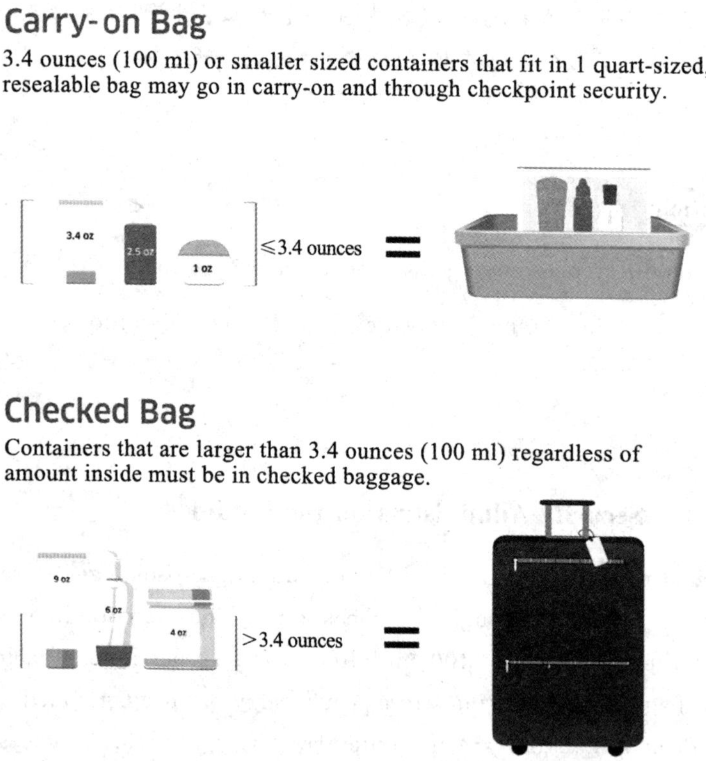

Pic. 1-4

The liquids are packed in a transparent, secure, tamper-evident bag by the retailer and do not show signs of tampering when presented to TSA for screening.

The original receipt for the liquids is present and the purchase was made within 48 hours.

The items inside the secure, tamper-evident bags must be screened and cleared. Any item that alarms or is unable to be screened will not be permitted in your carry-on bag. We recommend packing all liquids, gels, and aerosols that are over 3.4 oz or 100 ml in your checked baggage, even if they are in a secure, tamper-evident bag.

Liquids more than 3.4 oz or 100 ml not in a secure, tamper-evident bag must be packed in checked baggage.

(Adapted from *tas. gov*)

Part B After Boarding

B1. Introduction

Personal Health and Safety During and After Flight

Safety precautions

Reduce your chances of having a mishap during your trip by following a few simple safety precautions.

Wear a small travel bag during your flight that contains important items such as your wallet, passport, cash, emergency contact list, credit cards, and medication.

Don't leave gadgets or devices on your seat when you go to the bathroom.

Feel under your seat to locate the flotation device, and pay attention to the flight attendants' security briefing.

During the flight

Settle in, and place your most-needed items within easy reach. Make yourself comfortable in your loose-fitting clothing, and fill up your refillable water bottle early in the flight.

Remember that caffeinated, carbonated and alcoholic drinks are diuretics, so avoid consuming them during the flight. Herbal tea is a good alternative to coffee and caffeinated tea, so bring a few bags with you. Ginger tea can be especially good for nausea and motion sickness, and chamomile may help you fall asleep.

Avoid eating sugary and starchy foods, as well as foods that give you gas. Sugar can wreak havoc on your blood sugar levels, leaving you irritable and feeling hungry. If possible, snack on fresh fruits and vegetables, nuts, whole-grain crackers and popcorn.

Move around during the flight as much as you can. When possible, walk up and down the aisle. When this isn't an option, flex your calf muscles occasionally to keep the blood flowing and avoid clots.

If you experience ear pain during takeoff and landing, try chewing on gum or sucking on a sweet to help your ears to pop.

Skin can feel dry and taut in the low humidity of an airplane cabin. Consider bringing a sheet of mask for freshening up. Yes, you'll look a bit crazy for a few minutes, but chances are good that no one will be paying attention to you.

Finally, keep your hands as clean as possible. A quick coat of hand sanitizer and a tray wipe-down with your cleansing wipes may neutralize those germs that tend to concentrate in plane cabins.

After the flight

Having safely arrived at your destination doesn't mean you can forget about your health. In fact, there are a couple of important things you should do after touch down.

First, get some fresh air and sunshine (if possible) in the hours after your arrival. Some people swear by walking barefoot to feel grounded once more. Plan for a good night's sleep, and try to adjust to your new time zone as quickly as possible. It's tempting to nap in the middle of the day after a long flight, but resist the temptation, and you'll recover from jet lag much quicker.

(Adapted from *greenclaim.com*)

B2. Words and Expressions

Vocabulary

1. cabin /ˈkæbɪn/ *n.* 飞机座舱
2. aisle /aɪl/ *n.* (客机、电影院或教堂座席间的)走廊,过道
3. buckle /ˈbʌkl/ *v.* 扣上
4. turbulence /ˈtɜːbjələns/ *n.* 紊流,湍流
5. oxygen /ˈɒksɪdʒən/ *n.* 氧气
6. stow /stəʊ/ *v.* 收藏,收起
7. raft /ræft/ *n.* 充气筏,橡皮艇

In the Airplane	**机舱内部**
cabin service	机舱服务(清洁卫生等硬服务)
on-board service / in-flight service	机舱服务(餐饮等软服务)
find your seat	寻座
flight attendant	空乘服务员
overhead compartment	行李架
aisle	过道
window seat	靠窗座
middle / center seat	中间座
aisle seat	过道座
fasten / buckle your seat belt while seated	就座时紧扣安全带

call button	呼叫键
turbulence	紊流，湍流(由气体或水运动导致)
oxygen mask	氧气罩
emergency exit	紧急出口
tray table	托盘桌
table must be stowed	将桌子收起来
during taxiing, takeoff and landing	在飞机滑行、起飞和着陆期间
airsickness bag	呕吐袋
life vest / jacket under your seat	座椅下面的救生衣
life raft	救生艇

Vocabulary

1. runway /ˈrʌnəweɪ/ *n.* 跑道
2. terminal /ˈtɜːmɪnl/ *n.* 候机楼，航站楼
3. taxi /ˈtæksi/ *v.* 在地面滑行
4. schedule /ˈskedʒuːl/ *v.* 安排，排定
5. layover /ˈleɪoʊvər/ *n.* 飞机短暂停留
6. carousel /ˌkærəˈsel/ *n.* 行李传送器
7. transfer /ˈtrænsfɜːr/ *n.* 转乘，转乘费用
8. transit /ˈtrænzɪt/ *n.* 运输，输送
9. declare /dɪˈkler/ *v.* 申报物品价值

Landing	**飞机着陆**
runway	跑道
terminal (building)	航站楼
control tower	控制塔
take off	起飞
land / touch down	着陆
circle	盘旋
taxi in / out	滑行进入(出)跑道
scheduled time	预计抵达时间
actual time	实际抵达时间
layover	中途停留(几个小时)
stopover	中途停留(几天)

Baggage / Luggage Claim	**行李提取**
baggage claim area	行李提取处
luggage cart / trolley	行李车
baggage / luggage carousel	行李传送器
luggage claim check	行李提取检查
Lost & Found counter	失物招领处
make a lost luggage report	做失物登记
flight transfer	转机
transfer passengers	转机乘客
transfer correspondence	中转处前台
transfer hall	换乘大厅
connecting flight	衔接航班,换乘航班
transit visa	过境签证
transit counter	过境柜台
goods to declare	报关物品

Vocabulary

1. jetlagged /ˈdʒetˌlægd/ *adj*. 有时差的
2. duty /ˈdjuːti/ *n*. 关税
3. reservation /ˌrezərˈveɪʃn/ *n*. 预定,预约
4. package /ˈpækɪdʒ/ *v*. 将多种服务或产品打包销售
5. subway /ˈsʌbweɪ/ *n*. 地铁
6. coach /koʊtʃ/ *n*. 长途客车,大巴

Arrival	**抵达**
fill in (out) declaration form	填写报关单
money / currency exchange	货币兑换处
jetlag	时差
feel jetlagged	有时差感
greeting area	机场迎宾区
greeting arriving	迎接到来
baggage / luggage locker	行李柜
duty-free shop	免税店
hotel reservation	酒店预订
tour arrangement	旅游安排

packaged tour	旅行社包办的旅游项目
group tour	组团游，团游
ticket office	售票处
subway / rail pass	地铁通行证
taxi pick-up point	出租车接送点
airline coach service	机场大巴服务
car rental / hire	租车服务
driver license	驾照

Vocabulary

1. visa /ˈviːzə/ *n.* 签证
2. accompanying /əˈkʌmpənɪŋ/ *adj.* 陪伴的，随行的
3. destination /ˌdestɪˈneɪʃn/ *n.* 目的地，终点
4. issue /ˈɪʃuː/ *v.* 发行，颁发
5. itinerary /aɪˈtɪnərəri/ *n.* 旅行计划，预定行程
6. expiry /ɪkˈspaɪri/ *n.* 到期，期满

Visa	**签证**
family name / surname	姓氏
first (given) name	名
sex	性别
accompanying number	偕行人数
occupation	职业
nationality	国籍
passport No.	护照号
destination country	目的地国家
country of origin	始发国家
city where you boarded	登机城市
city where visa was issued	签证签发地
date issued	签发日期
address while in	前往国家的居住地址
official use only	官方填写
customs declaration	海关申报
immigration	入境(处)
itinerary	行程

I-20 form	留学生身份表
I-94 form	出入境表
expiry date	签证失效期
for stays of 3 months	有效期三个月

B3. Situational Conversations

Conversation 1 In-flight Instructions

FA: Flight Attendant P: Passenger

P: Would it be all right if I asked you a few questions about your in-flight instructions?

FA: I would love to help clarify any questions you might have.

P: When you were talking about the nearest exit, what were you talking about?

FA: There's a card in this seat pocket that shows you where your nearest exit is.

P: What if I need an oxygen mask?

FA: The oxygen mask is above you and will drop down if you need it.

P: Where are the life jackets?

FA: You will find your life jacket under your seat if you need it. Also, you have a seat cushion that can be used as a flotation device.

P: If I want to be safe, what can I do?

FA: Keep your seat belt fastened at all times. If you fall asleep, keep it fastened loosely around you in case we hit turbulence unexpectedly.

(Adapted from *eslfast.com*)

Conversation 2 Getting In-flight Services

The people who work inside the airplane serving food and drinks are called flight attendants. Both men and women who have this job are called flight attendants. The passengers are allowed to push the call button to get the attention of the flight attendant.

FA: Flight Attendant P: Passenger

FA: Yes? What can I do for you?

P: It's very cold in the cabin. Is it possible to get a blanket?

FA: We're out of blankets, but here's a pillow.

P: Okay, thanks. I was asleep during the meal service. Could I get a meal?

FA: We don't have any more of the Baked Chicken. We only have the Bean Salad left.

P: Oh, okay, I'll take that. Could I also get a drink?

FA: What would you like?

P: What do you have?

FA: The **complimentary drinks** are listed in our in-flight magazine. Beer, wine, and other cocktails are $4.

P: I'll have a diet soda.

FA: We're out of diet soda.

P: How about just some water? What's that?

FA: That's turbulence. Make sure your seat belt is fastened.

P: Could I get an airsickness bag, please?

FA: I'm sorry, but we're out of those, too.

(Adapted from *eslpod.com*)

☞**Note**

- **complimentary drinks**: It refers to drinks given or supplied without charge. If drinks, tickets, books, etc. are complimentary, they are given free, especially by a business. It can also be given free as a gift or courtesy. Complimentary drinks are commonly seen in hotel rooms with a complimentary tag as a reminder.

Conversation 3 Food Services

FA: Flight Attendant **P**: Passenger

FA: Chicken or pasta?

P: Sorry?

FA: Would you like chicken or pasta?

P: I'll have the chicken.

FA: Anything to drink?

P: What kind of soda do you have?

FA: Coke, Diet Coke, Sprite, Orange, and Dr. Pepper.

P: A Diet Coke, no ice, please.

FA: Here you go.

P: Thanks.

(Adapted from *espressoenglish.net*)

☞ **Notes**

- If you didn't understand what the flight attendant said, you can say "Sorry?" or "Pardon?" to ask him or her to repeat it.
- If you want to ask for something, you can use the phrase "Can I have... ?" or "Could I have... ?". Practice your pronunciation with these common requests:

  "Can I have a pillow?"

  "Can I have a blanket?"

  "Can I have a pair of headphones / earbuds?"

  "Could I have some water / coffee / tea?"

  "Could I have some extra napkins?"

B4. Picture Knowledge

Parts of an Aircraft

aeroplane (UK) airplane (US)

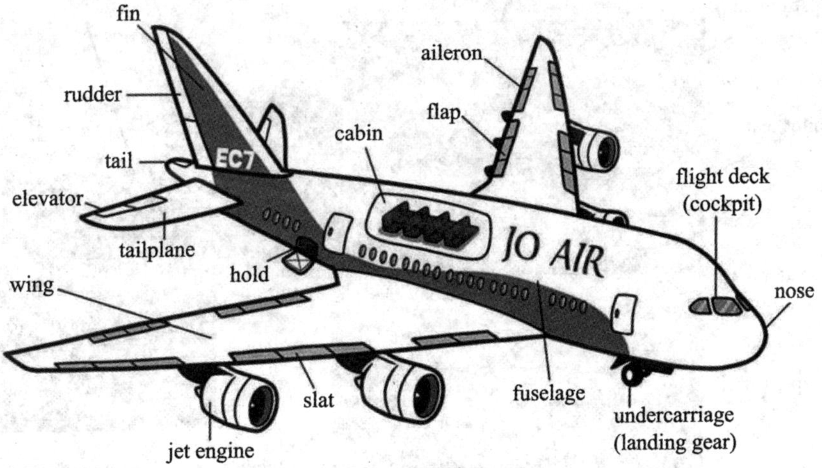

Pic. 1-5

Form 1-94 Arrival-Departure Card

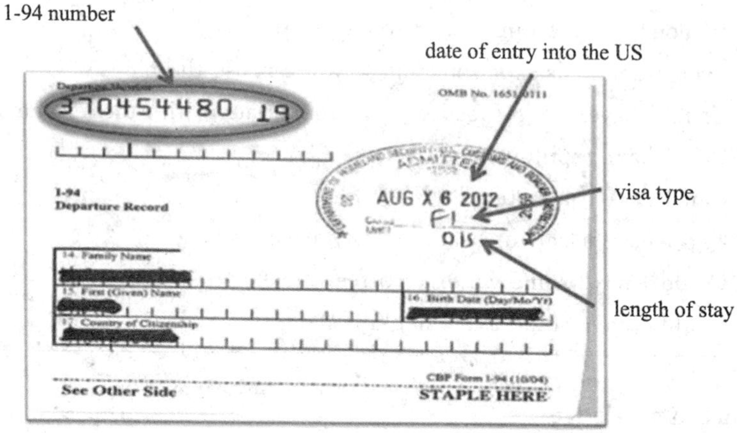

Pic. 1-6

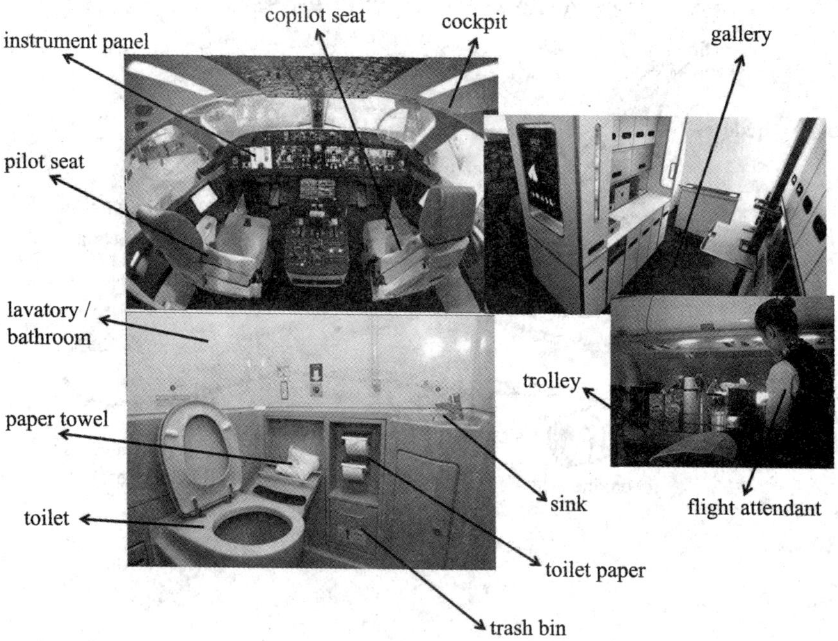

Pic. 1-7

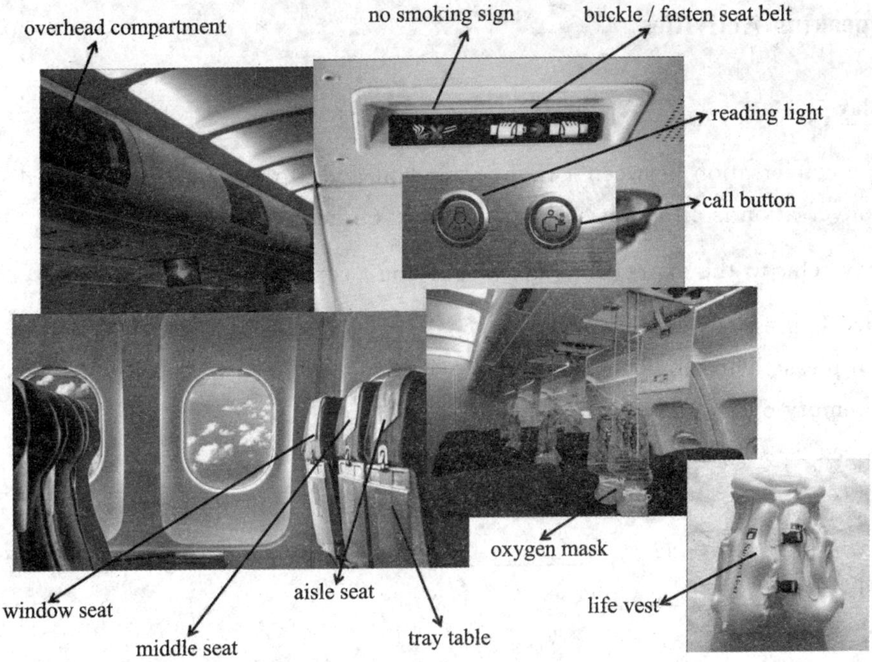
overhead compartment
no smoking sign
buckle / fasten seat belt
reading light
call button
window seat
middle seat
aisle seat
tray table
oxygen mask
life vest

Pic. 1-8

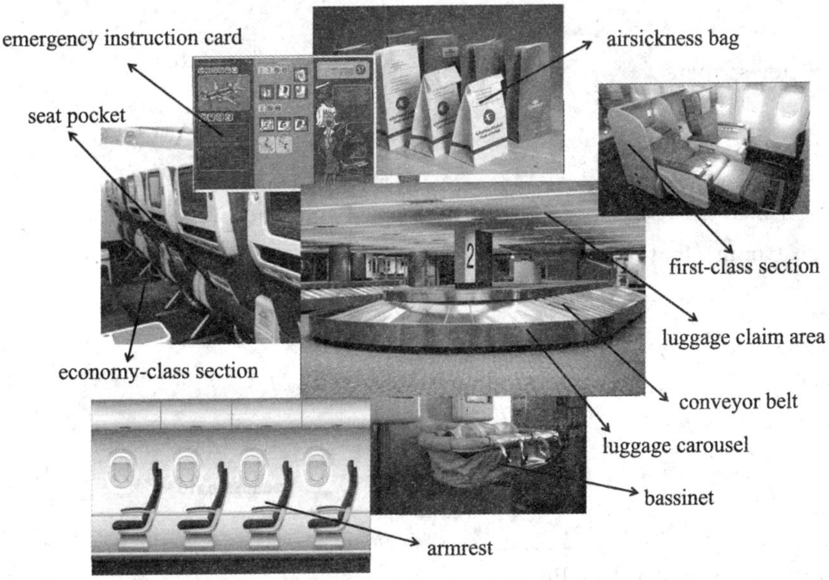
emergency instruction card
airsickness bag
seat pocket
first-class section
luggage claim area
economy-class section
conveyor belt
luggage carousel
bassinet
armrest

Pic. 1-9

B5. Speaking Activities

Role Play

Design a conversation between a flight attendant and a passenger for on-board service, your conversation is all about seeking services you need on board.

You may refer to the expressions below but don't confine yourself to them.

Suggested Expressions:

Can you please help me __________?
find an empty overhead bin
fit this bag
lift this carry-on

Could you please get me (a) __________ / may I have (a) __________, please? / I would like (a)__________, please.
blanket
pillow
headphones
bottled water
snacks
magazines / newspapers
earplugs
eye mask

Excuse me, where is the __________ / where can I find the __________?
lavatory / restroom / bathroom
galley
emergency exit
sickness bag
headphone jack
USB port

Can I __________? / May I __________?
use cell phone / laptop / tablet PC
unbuckle the seat belt
open the overhead bin
go to the restroom now
put down the armrest
recline my seat

Excuse me, how do I ________?
turn on the reading light
adjust the air vent

Please wake me up for service.
Please don't wake me up during this flight.
Please only wake me up for ________.

(Adapted from *guruin. com*)

Sentence Making

Imagine that you have a kid aged 2, you need to communicate with the flight attendant for your food, then use the words below to make several sentences into a full paragraph, which demonstrates how passenger asks for in-flight service.

You may refer to the expressions below but don't confine yourself to them.

Suggested Expressions:

Excuse me, ________?
call button
mashed potato
apple crush
chewy gum
sickness bag
chicken noodle
disposal fork and spoon
coffee (Cappuccino, Latte, Americano, or Espresso)
napkin
wipes

Retelling

Read the story below and retell it to the class with details.

Night Flight

Simon Collings

The flight is busy and the last few passengers to board are searching for places to stow their hand luggage. The Asian woman in the seat next to me is in her late twenties, probably travelling on business. She's wearing an expensive perfume which seems familiar though I can't quite place it. I am wondering if I should talk to her when the man in the window seat shows up and we have to let him in. She settles back in the middle seat. When I try to strap myself back in I find she's picked up the buckle of my belt by accident and we look at each other and laugh.

"What have you been doing in Bangalore?" I ask.

"My office is there. It's where I'm based." She has a North American accent without a trace of the English as spoken in the subcontinent. She tells me she works for a multinational company that makes clothing and that she is on her way to Thailand. She has to visit a couple of factories and meet with some other people from the company. She's also trying to complete her PhD thesis, which is on a laptop she has under the seat in front of her. She has a fine silver ring on the third finger of her left hand. While she's talking, she puts her passport away in her bag and I see she's Canadian.

She asks me what I do and I tell her. Then I ask her some more about her job and she tells me about that. By this time, we are in the air and climbing towards our cruising altitude. The cabin is quiet, lights still dimmed, just the gentle sound of the air conditioning and the murmur of conversations. The flight to Singapore is three and a half hours. I can't decide whether to attempt sleep. It is nearly midnight and it hardly seems worth it.

(Adapted from *eastoftheweb.com*)

Interpretation

Interpret the following paragraphs into English with what you have learned in Part B.

Paragraph 1

张先生一登机便找到座位。他呼唤一名空乘服务员帮他将行李放在架子上后，就坐在靠窗座上。他细心检查了座椅下的救生衣，系好安全带，放下托盘桌，备好呕吐袋，又在脑海中确认了一遍紧急出口的位置，这才取了一份杂志阅读起来。不到五分钟，他又拿出旅游安排表，将酒店预订、门票购买等花费再核对一遍，以确认自己是否需要去货币兑换处换些美元。就在他绞尽脑汁地计算时，航站楼已出现在机窗外了。

Paragraph 2

王先生一下飞机就感觉到了时差。他先拉着行李车去行李提取处提取个人物件。然后，他在过境柜台办理过境签证，并填写了报关单。他想为家人购置一些礼品，便去免税店买东西，但发现自己没有当地货币。他只好去货币兑换处兑换一些货币，然后在机场迎宾区吃了饭。看到酒店预订和旅游安排的广告，王先生准备参加组团游。因为没有驾照，租车服务又太贵，他便在地铁售票处买了地铁通行证。

Paragraph 3

Paul 办理完行李托运，通过安检，准备从伦敦飞纽约。然而，机场突然通知他的航班延误了。幸好候机大厅有免费无线网，还可以逛一逛免税店。等了两个小时，Paul 终于办理了登机手续并顺利登机。很快，飞机在跑道上滑行并成功起飞。行程中，飞机遭遇了湍流，让他一直想呕吐，幸好飞机上有呕吐袋。熬过数个小时，终于要着陆了，飞机在纽约上空盘旋并进入跑道。航班的实际抵达时间比预计晚了 3 个小时。Paul 感到了时差，需要时间适应。倒霉的是，他的驾照丢了，不得不去失物招领处做失物登记。他的朋友 Tom 来接机，在出租车接送点叫了出租，并送他去酒店。

B6. Extension

Synonym Discrimination

Can you figure out the differences among the words below?

Group 1：handkerchief / napkin / tissue / toilet paper / wipes / paper towel
Group 2：cabin service / in-flight service / on-board service

Extensive Reading

Passage One

In-flight Medical Emergencies：A Review

Christian Martin-Gill，Thomas J. Doyle and Donald M. Yealy

Abstract

In-flight medical emergencies (IMEs) are common and occur in a complex environment with limited medical resources. Health care personnel are often asked to assist affected passengers and the flight team，and many have limited experience in this environment.

Observations

In-flight medical emergencies are estimated to occur in approximately 1 per 604 flights，or 24 to 130 IMEs per 1 million passengers. These events happen in a unique environment，with airplane cabin pressurization equivalent to an altitude of 5000 to 8000 ft during flight，exposing patients to a low partial pressure of oxygen and low humidity. Minimum requirements for emergency medical kit equipment in the United States include an automated external defibrillator；equipment to obtain a basic assessment，hemorrhage control，and initiation of an intravenous line；and medications to treat basic conditions.

Other countries have different minimum medical kit standards，and individual airlines have expanded the contents of their medical kit. The most common IMEs involve syncope or near-syncope (32.7%) and gastrointestinal (14.8%)，respiratory (10.1%)，and cardiovascular (7.0%) symptoms. Diversion of the aircraft from landing at the scheduled destination to a different airport because of a medical emergency occurs in an estimated 4.4% (95% CI, 4.3%-4.6%) of IMEs. Protections for medical volunteers who respond to IMEs in the United States include a Good Samaritan provision of the *Aviation Medical Assistance Act* and components of the *Montreal Convention*, although the duty to respond and legal protections vary across countries. Medical volunteers should identify their background and skills, perform an assessment, and report findings to ground-based medical support personnel through the flight crew. Ground-based recommendations ultimately guide interventions on board.

Conclusions and relevance

In-flight medical emergencies most commonly involve near-syncope and gastrointestinal, respiratory, and cardiovascular symptoms. Health care professionals can assist during these emergencies as part of a collaborative team involving the flight crew and ground-based physicians.

(Adapted from *nih.gov*)

Passage Two

How to Handle an In-flight Emergency

Lizzie Porter

The in-flight briefing

There is no legal requirement for staff to make passengers listen to the in-flight safety announcements that take place at the beginning of every flight. Those who do not follow the instructions are responsible for their own fate. However, cabin crew can intervene if rowdy passengers are preventing others from listening.

Life jackets

Staff learn emergency procedures inside out, but as a passenger, do you check your life jacket is actually there? Although spares are available on board, it is not a routine BA cabin crew requirement to make sure each seat has its inflatable. If you want to be able to don it immediately in the case of an emergency, it's up to you to check it's stowed where it should be. And no, First Class passengers do not have their own parachutes.

Types of emergency landings

In terminology that perhaps sounds paradoxical, emergency landings can be "planned" or "unplanned". The former is when cabin crew know something bad is going to happen —you are going to have to make an emergency landing because of fire or engine failure, for example. The latter is when it just does, without warning — in the event of a terrorist attack, for instance.

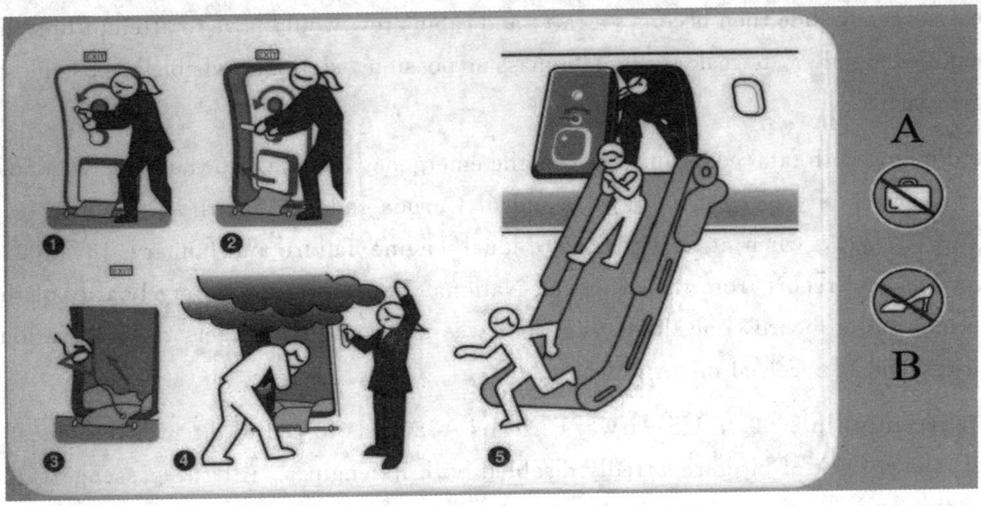

Pic. 1-10

Evacuation slides

The emergency slides that you hope you never have to use can be "lethal weapons", according to James Austin, a British Airways training executive.

If members of cabin crew haven't made sure the door is in manual on landing, the slide will inflate in less than 10 seconds, and ground staff on the other side of the door "won't be there much longer," James adds.

In an emergency, if passengers are refusing to get out, staff need to be prepared to do anything to get them onto the slide, including pushing, kicking, and shouting. It is their responsibility to get people out, and there is no time to accommodate those with vertigo. At full pelt, 150 people can be off in 60 seconds. The crew would also check the flight deck before leaping for the slide themselves. James explains: "If they've got us down, it might be nice to make sure they are alive." For security reasons, staff are not allowed to reveal other emergency circumstances in which crew would be allowed onto the flight deck.

Landing on water

"Ditchings", as landings on water are sometimes known, should only be attempted if there is no other emergency landing option, in situations, for example, when fuel runs out or becomes contaminated.

To prepare the cabin for this type of evacuation, crew would need to instruct them to put on any available clothes, to improve chances of survival in the water, and secure loose items: once water enters the fuselage, any floating objects could impede evacuation. A reminder of the step we hear so often —"in the event of an emergency, do not inflate your life jacket until outside the aircraft"— would be given.

The emergency slide then becomes a raft, and cabin crew would have to attempt link the inflatables together, to make as large a mass as possible, so it is as visible as possible to search parties.

One ditching with fatal consequences was the emergency landing into the Bengawan Solo River near the city of Solo on Java Island of Garuda Indonesia Airlines flight 421, a Boeing 737-300, when it experienced a dual engine failure on January 16, 2002. According to a report from the American National Transportation Safety Board, of the 60 occupants on board, one flight attendant was killed, 12 passengers received serious injuries, and 10 received minor injuries.

More recently, in 2009, a US Airways Airbus A320 was forced to ditch in the Hudson river after a flock of birds reportedly disabled both its engines. All 155 passengers and crew survived.

But what if you don't want to get people off the plane? James continues: "if you start an evacuation too soon and someone gets sucked into an engine, that's not a good day, is it?" If the surrounding environment is downright dangerous (on fire, stormy sea, a hostile terrain, say), it might be safer to stay in the plane.

On board fires

Next up, fire. British Airways trainees have a full day on this, since they must be prepared to fight everything from a wisp of smoke escaping from an in-flight entertainment screen, to a potential explosion.

British Airways staff admit that "due to the associated electricals," plane seats can and do catch fire, although they are cagey about how often this actually happens. If there was a serious combustion on board, however, the smoke could be so toxic that two, three or four breaths could kill; if all flammable materials on board ignited, temperatures would reach 1,000C, and passengers would be unlikely to survive.

So would staff tell passengers if there was a fire on board? It would depend on size and location. If the fire was near them, in a door panel or in their seat, then obviously yes, but if it was in the galley, then they needn't be any the wiser....

British Airways cabin crew trainees learn the ropes in a smoke-filled chamber, and are taught how to don the gas masks staff are equipped with for fire-related emergencies.

Passengers are advised to count the number of rows from their seat to the nearest exit. After joining trainees in the smoke chamber, it was easy to see why — I was completely disorientated. The smoke was not toxic, but my eyes still stung as we clambered to the exit.

Putting on the staff gas mask, I felt like Darth Vader. Why don't passengers get them? I asked. Apparently they are reserved for those actually fighting the fire.

Statistics on how often there is a serious fire on a plane are hard to come by. A 2002 report, however, suggested that, from the time of the first indication that there is a fire on board, crew have an average of 17 minutes to get a plane to the ground. Whether the fire is in the engine, the cabin, or is hidden (the most dangerous type of fire, as the delay in confirming its existence may allow it to spread), pilots are advised to land the plane as soon as possible.

Passengers might not have a gas mask in the event of a fire, but cabin crew come up against nastier on-board challenges when they are least well prepared — including exploding coffee machines.

The UK Flight Safety Committee, an association of professionals who seek to improve commercial aviation safety, in March reported a note from the Aviation Safety Reporting System, a NASA body that reports safety incidents, that detailed an accident with an exploding coffee machine that took place in January 2014. The flight had to be diverted and a member of cabin crew received second degree burns to face and chest when they "lifted the handle of the coffee maker and hot coffee grounds exploded out onto my chest and face."

Sick pilots

Finally, what would happen if the pilot was taken ill during the flight, and couldn't land the plane? Late last year, Mike Gongol, an off-duty American Air Force pilot responded to the Tannoy announcement: "Are there any non-revenue pilots on board?", and landed United Airlines flight 1637 on its way from Des Moines, in Iowa, to Denver, in Colorado. The pilot had suffered a cardiac event and now MrGongol was going to have to land the plane. British Airways said that for long-haul flights they have up to four people able to fly the plane on board, so should a similar emergency occur, passengers shouldn't have to take to the flight deck.

Emergencies on planes are, thankfully, not an every-flight occurrence, but if there's one thing worth remembering it's this: make sure you know where your life jacket is.

(Adapted from *traveller.com*)

Sources of Pictures

Pic. 1-1 Edited and processed by authors
Pic. 1-2 Edited and processed by authors
Pic. 1-3 Edited and processed by authors
Pic. 1-4 Retrieved from *tsa.com*
Pic. 1-5 Retrieved from *pinterest.com*

Pic. 1-6 Retrieved from *slideshare. net*
Pic. 1-7 Edited and processed by authors
Pic. 1-8 Edited and processed by authors
Pic. 1-9 Edited and processed by authors
Pic. 1-10 Retrieved from *thumbs-prod. si-cdn. com*

References

Christian Martin-Gill , Thomas J. Doyle and Donald M. Yealy. (2018). In-flight Medical Emergencies: A Review. *National Library of Medicine*. Retrieved from https://pubmed. ncbi. nlm. nih. gov/30575886/on July 29th, 2020.

Joshua Bote. (2019). A Man Tried to Smuggle $33,000 of Cocaine under His Wig. *Usatoday*. Retrieved from https://www. usatoday. com/story/news/world/2019/07/16/man-wig-hiding-cocaine-pound-airport-barcelona-spain/1742478001/on July 29th, 2020.

Lisa Maloney, Leaf Group. (2018). Tips for Attention before Check in. *Usatoday*. Retrieved from https://traveltips. usatoday. com/check-international-flights-39855. html/on July 29th, 2020.

Lizzie Porter. How to Handle an In-flight Emergency. *Traveller*. Retrieved from https://pubmed. ncbi. nlm. nih. gov/30575886/on July 29th, 2020.

Pahal Nopani. (2019). Personal Health and Safety during and after Flight. *Greenclaim*. Retrieved from https://www. greenclaim. com/blog/2019/02/28/7-things-to-pay-attention-to-during-a-long-haul-flight/on July 29th, 2020.

Security Administration for Liquid. *Official Website of the Department of Homeland Security*, *Britishairways*, *Euroairport*. Retrieved from https://www. tsa. gov/travel/security-screening/liquids-rule/; https://www. britishairways. com/jba/ba/fi _ FI/baggage/banned _ baggag. html/; https://www. euroairport. com/en/passengers-visitors/arrivals-departures/security-checks/liquids-gels-pastes. html/on July 29th, 2020.

At the Check-in Desk, Going through Security, Announcements at the Gate. *Espressoenglish*. Retrieved from https://www. espressoenglish. net/travel-english-conversations-in-the-airport/on July 29th, 2020.

In-flight Instructions. *Eslfast*. Retrieved from https://www. eslfast. com/robot/topics/travel/travel13. htm/on July 29th, 2020.

Simon Collings. Night Flight. *Eastoftheweb*. Retrieved from http://www. eastoftheweb. com/short-stories/UBooks/NighFlig927. shtml/on July 29th, 2020.

Getting In-flight Services. *Eslpod*. Retrieved from https://secure3. eslpod. com/podcast/esl-podcast-362-getting-in-flight-service/on July 29th, 2020.

Getting In-flight Services, Food Services. *Espressoenglish*. Retrieved from https://www. espressoenglish. net/travel-english-conversations-in-the-airport/on July 29th, 2020.

Unit 2 Accommodation

Part A On Campus

A1. Introduction

On-campus Housing

Students can immerse themselves in university life by staying in a residence hall or apartment on campus. You'll be just a short walk from classrooms, libraries, computing centers, cafés and other facilities. Universities or colleges offer residential halls or apartments that come fully equipped with almost everything you need to be comfortable and productive. Some universities require all entering first-year students to live in on-campus housing during their first one or two years of enrollment.

To apply for housing on campus, you will need to set up your Net ID of the university, and follow the instructions that come with your offer of admission. Once you have your Net ID, go to the Application and Assignment home page to begin the application process. The earlier you submit your application, the better the chance of getting your preferred location.

Residence hall living

You can reserve a room. Both one-person and two-person rooms are available. If you reserve a two-person room, you may request a specific roommate. Otherwise, a roommate will be assigned to you. In some universities, the housing office randomly assigns a residence hall and roommate for new first-year and transfer students, taking into consideration any special living opportunities and mutual roommate requests. The random housing assignment system is designed to promote a fair and equitable system for all new students and encourages students from different backgrounds to live together. Also, a meal plan is usually required for all students living in residence halls.

In most cases, rooms are furnished with extra-long twin-sized beds, desks, bookcases, chairs, dressers and closets. Small refrigerators may be rented for an additional charge. You will need to bring your own bedding, pillows and towels, unless they are included in your housing package.

You are responsible for cleaning your own room and washing your own towels and linens. Laundry facilities are available in each of the residence halls. Bathrooms and other shared facilities are cleaned regularly by custodial staff.

Apartment living

Apartment buildings are also available on campus. They offer single rooms in shared apartments. Some feature furnished two or four-bedroom apartments with fully equipped kitchens and shared bathrooms — one bathroom for every two bedrooms. There are also studio apartments with private bathrooms or furnished four or six-bedroom apartments with fully equipped kitchens, shared bathrooms and a community center. You can arrange to live with specific roommates. A meal plan is not required. We can get a glimpse of housing types and rates, taking Syracuse University for example.

Residence Hall		**Apartment**	
Room type	Rate(per student per semester)	Room type	Rate (per student per semester)
1-person suite	$5,920	1-bedroom apartment (1 student per apartment)	$5,660
large single	$5,310	2-bedroom apartment (2 students per apartment)	$5,260
single with bath	$5,310	3-bedroom apartment (3 students per apartment)	$4,855

* Syracuse University offers more room types of residence hall, such as regular single and 2-person suite.

In a nutshell, the on-campus housing application includes the following steps. Apply for on-campus living, receive one's housing assignment based on your requests and availability, sign housing contract online, and an automatic email will be sent to you to confirm your housing contract, then you are assigned to either single, double or triple rooms. In case you are assigned to the latter two, you are automatically matched with a roommate or roommates on the basis of lifestyle preference you completed in the housing application.

(Adapted from *ielp.uw.edu*, *syracuse.edu*)

A2. Words and Expressions

Vocabulary

1. hub /hʌb/ *n.* 中心，枢纽
2. sorority /səˈrɔːrəti/ *n.*（北美某些大学的）女生联谊会
3. fraternity / frəˈtɜːnəti / *n.*（北美某些大学的）男生联谊会

Housing Options	住宿选择
typical dorm rooms	典型的宿舍房间
residence halls	学生宿舍
singles and doubles	单人间和双人间
triples and quads	三人间和四人间
suites with multiple bedrooms	拥有多个卧室的套房
campus townhomes and apartments	校园联排别墅和公寓
language house / language immersion residence	（为语言学习者提供的）语言浸入式住宅
theme housing	主题住宅（如艺术主题住宅，多用于临时或短期住宿）
sorority house	（女大学生住在一起的）女生联谊住宅
fraternity house	（男大学生住在一起的）男生联谊住宅
single-sex housing	单性别住宅
co-ed housing	男女同住的住宅
gender-neutral housing	不分性别的住房
sundeck	（房屋周围的）露天平台
do a campus visit	访问校园
do an overnight stay	过夜
walk you through the campus	（别人）带你逛一下校园
give preference to certain room types	偏爱某些房型
become a social hub	成为社交中心

Vocabulary

1. virtual /ˈvɜːtʃuəl / *adj*. (通过计算机)虚拟的,网络的
2. lottery /ˈlɑːtəri/ *n*. 抽奖,彩票
3. immunization /ˌimjənəˈzeɪʃən/ *n*. 免疫接种

Housing Management	**住宿管理**
offer a virtual tour	提供网上虚拟参观
prior to arrival	在到达之前
housing assignment	住房分配
residential life office	住宿管理办公室
residential assistant	住宿管理员
hold housing lotteries	通过抓阄选房
familiarize oneself with check-in information	让自己熟知入住信息
comply with housing policies	遵守住宿政策
immunization requirement	接种疫苗的要求
provide routine maintenance for free	免费提供日常维护
under renovations	正在装修
conduct end-of-year inspections	进行年终检查
The room layouts differ.	房间布局不同。
Split the room, split the bill.	共享房间,共享账单。
First come, first served.	先到先得。
You strike gold in the housing lottery.	你的抓阄选房中了上上签。
Upperclassmen have first pick.	高年级学生优先选择。
Freshmen settle for the leftovers.	新生挑选剩下的。

Vocabulary

1. accessible /əkˈsesəbəl/ *adj*. 可进入的,可接近的,可得到的
2. communal /ˈkɑːmjənəl/ *adj*. 共同的,公用的
3. laundromat /ˌlɑːnˈdret/ *n*. 洗衣店(多指自助洗衣店)

Housing Conditions	**住宿条件**
wheelchair-accessible housing	可供轮椅通行的住宅

substance-free housing	禁酒精饮品及违规药品的社区住宅（主要面向留学生）
have guaranteed privacy	拥有隐私保证
house up to five or six students	容纳五六个学生
share a communal bathroom	共用一个公共浴室
big enough to fit dressers	大到可以放下梳妆台
laundromat	洗衣店(多指自助洗衣店)
do the laundry	洗衣服
coin-operated laundry	投币洗衣房
front loading washing machine	前装式洗衣机
insert quarters or slide a card	插入硬币或刷卡
mail and package delivery service	邮件及包裹递送服务
vending area	自动售货区
fitness center	健身中心
bicycle storage	自行车存放(处)
accommodate students' streaming needs	满足学生的流媒体需求
place shuttle stops nearby	在附近设置摆渡车站
meet one's transportation need	满足学生的交通需求
purchase a parking permit	购买停车许可证
One's car should match his parking tag.	车辆必须与停车牌吻合。
The room comes furnished with the bare bones.	房间只有基本家具和陈设。

Vocabulary

1. foyer /ˈfɔɪeɪ/ *n.* (剧院、宾馆等公共建筑物入口内的)门厅
2. theft /θeft/ *n.* 盗窃，偷窃行为
3. receptacle /rɪˈseptəkəl/ *n.* 容器，贮存器
4. disposal /dɪˈspoʊzəl/ *n.* 处理，清除；可供使用

Amenities and Facilities	**便利设施**
dining hall	餐厅
make meal plans	制订就餐计划
self-catering	自理膳食的
kitchenette	小厨房
individual toilet stall	独立卫生间
recreation area	娱乐休闲区

foyer / lobby	门厅
common room	公共休息室
wireless internet access	无线上网
adequate Wi-Fi capabilities	充足的无线局域网服务
cable television package	有线电视套餐
storage locker	储物柜
receptacles for convenient disposal	便于处置废弃物或回收品的容器
fire alarm	消防报警器
smoke detector	烟感器
sprinkler system	消防喷淋系统
fire exit / emergency stairway	消防出口
garbage chute	垃圾道
central heating	集中供暖
intercom / speaker	对讲系统
The toilet clops.	马桶堵了。
The pipe bursts.	水管爆了。
You may contact the office at ext. 7777.	你可以拨打分机号码 7777 与办公室联系。

A3. Situational Conversations

Conversation 1　A Tour with the Resident Assistant

A resident assistant is showing a high school student around in the residence hall.

RA: Resident Assistant　S: Student

RA: Good morning and welcome to our residence hall.

S: Thank you. I really appreciate your time.

RA: You are welcome. First let me give you a brief intro of this hall. It's in memory of Mrs. Jones, one of the most generous **benefactors** in our university's history. It houses only undergraduates, with a capacity of 200 current students; there are different room types, 1-person rooms, 2-person rooms, suites and so on.

S: Cool! Could I take a look at the room?

RA: Sure thing. A-103 is not occupied right now, and it's the first on the right. As you can see, it's a 1-person suite, provided with a bed, desk, desk chair, dresser and closet. One just gets bedding ready when moving in.

S: Impressive. Where am I supposed to take a bath?

RA: There's a **communal bathroom** at the end of corridor and there are shower stalls for residents. Just have a look at the times when they are available. And don't be ashamed to play music while you're showering.

S: Can I cook for myself in the building?

RA: There are communal kitchen facilities, including microwave ovens, in all residences. Dishes, utensils, and cookware are not provided, and you should bring your own. Cooking is NOT permitted in residents'rooms. Residents may rent an approved MicroFridge for use in their room.

S: Will I have laundry facilities?

RA: There are washers and dryers in each residence or complex.

S: How can I live in such a room, I mean, could I reserve one beforehand?

RA: Definitely. Frankly speaking, it's very popular with first-year students. You know, privacy and space, things like that.

S: OK, I see. What's the housing application like?

RA: Just follow the brochure for the first-year students. You should first register, set up your Campus ID of the university. You can also call 3456-789 to get help from Students' Housing Office.

S: Thanks! I wanna take a look at the floor **lounge**. Where is it?

RA: OK. This way, please. It's communal. Everyone can come, sit and study. The lounge is a magical place. It's one of the best places to study and socialize, because you can help each other with work while being in a social environment.

S: Thank you. And now I have some ideas about the residence hall. It seems like a cool and fun place. I can't wait to reserve one if I'm admitted into this university.

RA: Yeah, it helps to connect with your fellow students and make your time on campus meaningful and productive.

S: Thanks again.

RA: Not at all. Glad I can help. Wish you have some quality time on campus.

☞**Notes**

- **resident assistant:** A part-time student paraprofessional position within the Office of Residence Life and Housing, a unit of Student Affairs. The RA is responsible for performing a variety of front desk, clerical, and customer service functions.
- **benefactor:** Someone who gives money for a good purpose.
- **communal bathroom:** The bathroom shared by a group of people who live together.
- **lounge:** A public room in a hotel or other building. It is used by many people as a place to relax.

Conversation 2 Housing Arrangements

A student and a residence hall counselor are talking about changing housing arrangements.

S: Student C: Counselor

S: Excuse me. Who should I see about changing my housing arrangements?

C: Hello. I'm the person. But making a change in the middle of the term is not all that easy. You've got to have a pretty good reason.

S: I don't think it would be easy, but if I don't do something, I'm going to fail half of my courses this term.

C: That does sound serious. What's the problem?

S: Well, my roommate is nice enough, but he **burns the midnight oil**, staying up awfully late at night either reading or just listening to music.

C: That doesn't sound that bad. Believe me, I've heard a lot worse.

S: I don't think you're getting the whole picture yet. My roomie is up till two or three in the morning every single night.

C: He must be pretty tired during the day then.

S: I don't know. Maybe he takes naps, or maybe he doesn't need as much sleep as others. I really don't care how he does it. I just want to be moved out of that room, because I know I can't live that way.

C: OK. It's not the kind of problem we would normally move someone for, but if you fill out this application for a hardship housing relocation, I'll see what I can do.

S: How long do you think it will take?

C: Don't worry. We try to take actions very quickly if there's a real problem; several days at most, uh... for the most urgent cases anyway. I'm not even sure I'll be able to get you moved out at all.

S: Do I have any other options?

C: The only one I can think of is moving off campus. You're not a freshman, are you?

S: No, I'm in my second year.

C: Then you could look for off-campus housing.

S: But if I did that, I'd have to **forfeit** all the money I paid for housing this term, wouldn't I?

C: Not necessarily. In a situation like yours, we'll often refund the housing costs for the reminder of the term and let you move out. To be honest, I really don't think you'll qualify for immediate on-campus relocation. But you might qualify for the refund.

S: Now I **get the picture**. Thank you so much.

C: You're welcome.

(Adapted from *TOEFL iBT*)

☞**Notes**

- **burn the midnight oil**: (*Informal*) to work or study until late at night.
- **forfeit**: To lose a right, position, possession etc. or have it taken away from you because you have broken a law or rule.
- **get the picture**: (*Informal*) to understand a situation.

Conversation 3 Meal Plan

A student is talking to a personnel from the Dining Services of the university about meal plan.

S: Student P: Personnel

S: Excuse me, I'm having a problem with my meal card.

P: Hello. How can I help?

S: Well, there must be some problem with my student ID card. I couldn't swipe it in the cafeteria last night.

P: Can I see your card, please? OK, just let me enter your card number into the computer. A cash register also shows available meals each time you use your card. It's always a good idea to keep track of your meal plan.

S: I've never done that.

P: It says here you purchased 12 meals per week and used the last one yesterday afternoon.

S: I did purchase 12 meals per week, but then I changed it to 14 meals per week not long ago.

P: That's the problem. The change isn't showing up in your account. There are no updates.

S: Well, the change was made and I can prove it. Here is the receipt for the additional payment.

P: Right.

S: What can I do about it now?

P: There are two options really. I can either make the change to your account now, so you'll have 14 meals per week for the rest of semester, or I can leave the account unchanged and refund to you the additional payment. It's your call.

S: Let me see. I prefer 14 meals peer week.

P: Alright. As a reminder, meals are not transferable and sharing someone's meal plan is not an option.

S: I understand. Thank you so much!

(Adapted from *TOEFL iBT*)

A4. Picture Knowledge

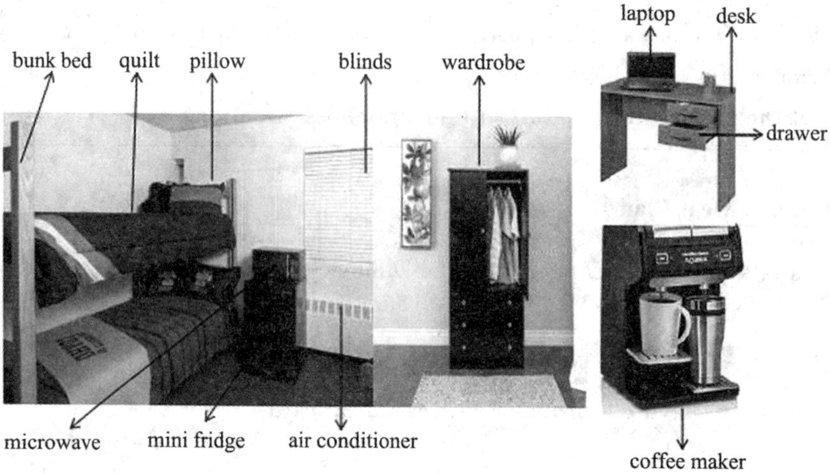

Pic. 2-1

A5. Speaking Activities

Role Play

Make a dialogue between a first-year student and a clerk for housing assignments. Your conversation should cover inquiries of room types, application, contract confirmation, amenities and facilities.

You may refer to the expressions below but don't confine yourself to them.

Suggested Expressions:

How are housing assignments made?
How are roommates matched up?
Why wasn't I assigned to the room type / building I requested?
May I request a different room assignment?
What if I don't like my room / building once I get to campus?
What if I have nothing in common with my roommate(s)?
What is my building / community like?
What will my room be like?
What will be provided in my room / suite / apartment?
Will I have laundry facilities in my building?
Will I need personal property insurance?
When should I move in, and how should I prepare?

What should I do if I have additional questions?

Discussion

You have five minutes to read the passage below, and then you are required to give some suggestions for getting along well with your roommates on campus.

Getting Along with Your College Roommate(s)

Kelci Lynn Lucier

You may have grown up living with lots of siblings, or this maybe your first time sharing your living space with someone else. While having a roommate inevitably has its challenges, it can also be a great part of your college experience. Follow these ten tips to make sure you and your roommate keep things pleasant and supportive throughout the year (or even years!).

Be clear about your expectations from the beginning

Do you know in advance that you hate it when someone hits the snooze button fifteen times every morning? That you're a neat freak? That you need ten minutes to yourself before talking to anyone after you wake up? Let your roommate know as soon as you can about your little quirks and preferences. It's not fair to expect him or her to pick up on them right away, and communicating what you need is one of the best ways to eliminate problems before they become problems.

Address problems when they're little

Is your roommate always forgetting her stuff for the shower, and taking yours? Are your clothes being borrowed faster than you can wash them? Addressing things that bug you while they're still little can help your roommate be aware of something she may not otherwise know. And addressing little things is much easier than addressing them after they've become big.

Respect your roommate's stuff

This may seem simple, but it's probably one of the biggest reasons why roommates experience conflict. Don't think he'll mind if you borrow his cleats for a quick soccer game? For all you know, you just stepped over an uncrossable line. Don't borrow, use, or take anything without getting permission first.

Be mindful of who you bring into your room — and how often

You may love having your study group into your room. But your roommate may not. Be mindful of how often you bring people over. If your roommate studies best in the quiet, and you study best in a group, can you alternate who hits the library and who gets the room?

Lock the door and windows

This may seem like it has nothing to do with roommate relationships, but how would you feel if your roommate's laptop got stolen during the ten seconds it took you to run down the hall? Or vice versa? Locking your door and windows is a critical part of keeping safe on campus.

Be friendly, without expecting to be best friends

Don't go into your roommate relationship thinking that you are going to be best friends for the time you're at school. It may happen, but expecting it sets both of you up for trouble. You should be friendly with your roommate but also make sure you have your own social circles.

Be open to new things

Your roommate may be from some place you've never heard of. They may have a religion or lifestyle that is completely different from your own. Be open to new ideas or experiences, especially as they relate to what your roommate brings into your life. That's why you went to college in the first place, right?

Stay open to change

You should expect to learn and grow and change during your time at school. And the same should happen to your roommate, if all goes well. As the semester progresses, realize things will change for both of you. Be comfortable addressing things that unexpectedly come up, setting new rules, and being flexible to your changing environment.

Address problems when they're big, too

You may not have been totally honest with tip 2, or you may suddenly find yourself with a roommate who goes wild after being shy and quiet the first two months. Either way, if something gets to be a big problem quickly, deal with it as soon as you can.

If nothing else, follow the golden rule

Treat your roommate like you'd like to be treated. No matter what your relationship is at the end of the year, you can take comfort knowing you acted like an adult and treated your roommate with respect.

Don't think you and your roommate are going to be able to work it out? It can be easier than you think to address your problems and, ideally, find a solution that works for both of you.

(Adapted from *thoughtco. com*)

Debate

At many American colleges and universities, students need to live in the residence halls for the first year or two, then they can choose to live off campus. A few schools require campus residency for all four years. What's your opinion? You will carry out a team debate on the topic: ***Live on campus or off campus***?

Try to seek diverse perspectives and don't confine yourself to the expressions below.

Suggested Expressions:

On-campus housing

proximity
independence
all utilities included
no security deposit
don't even need a car
tightly-knit community
a shorter commute
a stronger sense of community
easier to make connections with people

Off-campus housing

privacy
isolation
a sense of responsibility
extra or higher costs
much more freedom
may have more space
a longer commute
don't have strict rules over your head
may feel disconnected from campus life

Interpretation

Interpret the following paragraphs into English with what you have learned in Part A.

Paragraph 1

Paul是一名新生。昨天,他来到宿舍管理办公室,在宿舍工作人员的帮助下办理住宿事宜。他希望马上入住,但是烟雾报警器坏了,正在维修中。他决定先参观一下校园。在参观校园的路上,他发现教学楼和宿舍楼相距非常近,而且都有就餐区域,还提供自动售货机和微波炉,这给校园住宿带来了极大的便利,也是校园住宿的一大优势。他十分期待住校生活。

Paragraph 2

最近,我打算考研。为了集中精力备考,我决定搬到校外的公寓居住。很快,我在离校不远的地方找到了一个公寓小区。小区有一个休闲娱乐区，还有公共休息室、投币洗衣机和运动设施。这里的每套公寓都有很大的卧室、卫生间及阳台，因为不用跟他人分享任何空间，所以个人隐私能得到保障。公寓的一楼还有一个自动售货区域，便于租客们采购生活用品及食物。这个地方令我很满意，我决定马上签约并搬入。

Paragraph 3

Lee是刚毕业的大学生，想在海淀区租赁一间配备家具的小公寓。他希望小区附近有摆渡车站，小区有专用停车场、自行车停放处、健身中心及24小时便利店。公寓有一间会客厅、一间卧室、一间小厨房和独立卫生间。此外，公寓能够提供中央供暖、无线网，配置烟雾报警器和自动喷水灭火系统，以保障消防安全。Lee希望房东是个喜欢宠物的人，因为他有一只小猫和一只小狗。Lee不喜欢外卖，爱好烹饪，因此公寓需要配备基本的厨房用具。关于房租，他将与房东面议。

A6. Extension

Synonym Discrimination

Can you figure out the differences among the words below?
Group 1: canteen / cafeteria / diner / dining hall / food court
Group 2: dormitory / hall of residence

Extensive Reading

Passage One

What to Expect from College Meal Plan?

Allen Grove

One of the big differences between high school and college doesn't happen in the classroom, but at meal time. No longer will you eat meals around the family table. Instead, you'll make your own food choices in the college dining hall. To pay for your meals, chances are you'll need to purchase a meal plan for at least part of your college career. This article explores some of the questions you may have about these plans.

College meal plans

Most colleges require residential students to get a meal plan. This is especially true for first-year students. The price of meal plans will vary significantly from school to school and the type of plan. Options ranging from 7 to 21 meals a week may be available.

At most schools, your meal card will work at all dining facilities on campus giving you a wide range of options. At some schools, the money for unused meals can be spent at a campus convenience store or even with local merchants.

What is a meal plan?

Essentially, a meal plan is pre-paid account for your on-campus meals. At the start of the term, you pay for all the meals you'll eat in the dining halls. You'll then swipe your student ID or a special meal card every time you enter a dining area, and the value of your meal will be deducted from your account.

How much do meal plans cost?

Whenever you look at the cost of college, you'll need to factor in much more than tuition. Room and board costs vary widely, typically between $7,000 and $14,000 a year. Meals will often be half of that cost. Meal prices don't tend to be unreasonable, but they certainly aren't as cheap as making meals in your own kitchen. Colleges usually subcontract meal services to a for-profit company, and the college will also earn a percentage of the meal fees. Students who live off campus and enjoy cooking can often eat well and save money compared to a meal plan. At the same time, the convenience and variety of a meal plan have many advantages.

Do you need to buy a meal plan?

At most schools, first-year students are required to have a meal plan. This requirement might be waved if you are commuting from home. Mandatory meal plans have a variety of purposes. Schools often want first-year students to become engaged in the campus community, and on-campus meals play an important part in that process. It's also possible the requirement is coming from a contract with the food service provider, not the college itself. And, of course, the college makes money from the meal plan, so it benefits the schools bottom line when a plan is required.

Which meal plan should you get?

Most colleges offer many different meal plans—you may see options for 21, 19, 14, or 7 meals a week. Before purchasing a plan, ask yourself some questions. Are you likely to get up in time for breakfast? Are you likely to go out to the local pizza joint for dinner? Few students actually use 21 meals a week. If the reality is that you often skip breakfast and tend to eat pizza at one in the morning, then you might want to choose a less expensive meal plan and spend your saved money buying food at local eateries at the times that better match your habits.

What happens if you don't use all your meals?

This varies from school to school, but often unused meals are money lost. Depending on the plan, the credit for unused meals may disappear at the end of the week or the end of the semester. You'll want to check your balance frequently—some schools have small grocery stores where you can spend the money from unused meals. Some schools also have arrangements with local merchants, restaurants, and even farmers' market that make it possible to spend dining dollars off campus.

Should you get a bigger meal plan if you eat a lot?

Nearly all college campuses offer all-you-can-eat dining in at least some of the dining halls, so the same meal plan can accommodate you whether you eat like a mouse or a horse. Just watch out for that freshman 15—all-you-can-eat can be bad for your waistline! Nevertheless, athletes with giant appetites rarely complain about going hungry in college.

What can you do if you have special dietary needs?

When a college has thousands or tens of thousands of students, it is going to have many students who can't eat gluten, have dairy allergies, or are vegetarian or vegan. Food service providers at colleges are prepared to handle students' special dietary restrictions. Some schools even have entire dining halls dedicated to vegan and vegetarian options. At very small colleges, it's not unusual for students to develop relationships with the food service staff to have custom meals prepared for them.

When your friends or family visit, can they eat with you?

Yes. Most schools allow you to swipe in guests with your meal card. If not, your guests can always pay cash to eat in the dining hall.

(Adapted from *thoughtco. com*)

Passage Two

Reasons You're Required to Live on Campus for Your First Year of College

Allen Grove

At many colleges and universities, you will need to live in the residence halls for your first year or two of college. A few schools require campus residency for all four years. Even if your school allows students to live off campus, consider the pros and cons of living on campus before making a final decision.

Why you're required to live on campus for your first year of college

Students are most likely to stay at a college when they feel like they belong. This sense of belonging has a direct impact on a college's retention rate and graduation rate. When new students live off campus, they are less likely to get involved in campus clubs and activities and will have a harder time making friends among fellow students.

When a student lives on campus, the college has an easier time helping out should that student encounter trouble on the academic or social front. Resident Advisors (RAs) and Resident Directors (RDs) are trained to intervene and assist when students are struggling, and they can help direct students to the appropriate people and resources on campus.

A college education is about much more than taking classes and earning a degree. Residential life teaches many important life skills: resolving conflicts with a roommate, suitemates, and / or students on your hall; learning to live with people who may be quite different from you; building a living and learning community; and so on.

At most schools, campus residence halls are much closer to important facilities (library, gym, health center, etc.) than off-campus apartments.

Colleges have little ability to monitor illegal behavior off campus, but within the residence halls, activities such as underage drinking and illegal drug use can be detected and responded to much more readily.

When you are a new student, it can be a huge benefit to be living in the same building with upper-class students and / or RAs who know the campus and academic expectations well. You're also more likely to find mentors in a campus residence hall than in an off-campus apartment.

Along with having upper-class mentors, you'll also have a peer group that will include students taking some of the same classes as you. Living on campus gives you ready access to study groups, and peers can often help if you are forced to miss a class or if you find material from a lecture confusing.

Along with the obvious benefits of living on campus, colleges have a few reasons for keeping students on campus that may be a bit less altruistic. Specifically, colleges don't make all of their money from tuition dollars. For the great majority of schools, significant revenues also flow from room and board charges. If dorm rooms sit empty and not enough students are signed up for meal plans, the college will have a harder time balancing its budget. If more states move forward with free tuition plans for in-state students at public universities (such as New York's Excelsior Program), all college revenue will come from room, board, and associated fees.

Exceptions to college residency requirements

Keep in mind that very few colleges have residential policies that are set in stone, and exceptions are often made.

If your family lives very close to the college, you can often get permission to live at home. Doing so obviously has significant cost benefits, but don't lose sight of the valuable experiences you might miss out on by choosing to commute. By living at home, you won't be getting the full college experience, including learning how to be independent.

Some colleges with two-or three-year residency requirements allow strong students to petition to live off campus sooner. If you've proven your academic and personal maturity, you may be able to move off campus earlier than many of your classmates.

At some schools, it may also be possible to petition to live off campus for reasons related to specific health and wellness needs. For example, you might be able to petition to live off campus if the college can't meet your atypical dietary requirements or if you need access to regular health care that simply isn't feasible in a college residence hall.

A final word about residency requirements

Every college has residency requirements that were developed for the unique situation of the school. You'll find that some urban schools as well as some universities that have been experiencing rapid expansion, simply don't have enough dormitory space to handle all of their students. Such schools often cannot guarantee housing and may be happy for you to live off campus.

At any school, it's important to weigh the pros and cons of living off campus before making a decision. Time spent cooking meals and commuting to campus is time that won't be spent on your studies, and not all students do well with too much independence.

(Adapted from *thoughtco.com*)

Part B Off Campus

B1. Introduction

Off-campus Housing

As regards accommodations for those newly-admitted college students, there are usually two options, either living on or off campus. In American universities or colleges, usually it's a must to live in residence halls and apartments on campus or in the vicinity of the campus for the first year. It cannot be guaranteed that all applicants can live in the apartments managed by the university. You have to share a room with someone, and it costs you an arm and a leg to live on campus, one might say. So after some time students might choose off-campus housing. Here is a step-by-step guide to finding housing.

Before you go

Before you embark on your journey to America, the smart way to rent an apartment is to do your homework:

Contact student affairs office or housing office of your college. People there can recommend popular apartments and might already have a placement program which can assist you with the whole process. Some colleges even have lists of approved landlords, campus partners, property management companies or properties that previous students have rented. So you can find out which resources are available.

You can also check out the off-campus introduction on the homepage of your college. For example, newcomers can find Arrival & Survival on the homepage of University of Pittsburg, so that they know where they are going and what to do once they get there. There's no need to try to navigate on your own.

Apartment-finding websites are a reliable way to browse apartments for rent. There are some popular ones, such as rent. com, rentcollegepads. com, apartmentguide. com, apartmentfinder. com, zillow. com, craigslist. org, etc. You can sort by price or by distance from your college. There are usually good, clear pictures of the interiors and exteriors of the rentals, and you can generally find newly built or even fully furnished apartments.

Contact Chinese Students and Scholars Association (CSSA) of the college for more housing information. You can also join housing-related chat groups, because students are often in search of roommates there. If you're interested, you can reach them.

Time to lease

One is supposed to keep an eye on the time to lease. It might happen that the apartment you want is only available after the freshman orientation, then you have to think about temporary housing: staying in a hotel that can be rented daily or weekly or staying in a nightly suite that can be rented monthly.

Decide on an apartment

Once you find a few apartments you like, you'll need to choose among them by comparing the buildings in which they are located. Assessing an apartment building's location, amenities, and a few other features can help you pick out a great apartment. Of course, different people are looking for different types of apartments, so there's no such thing as a perfect building. Double check that the apartments you are interested in meet your budget requirements. Be sure to factor in additional costs for utilities, parking, and laundry. Figure out what you're looking for most in your apartment building, and evaluate them accordingly.

Evaluating transit and parking. Having a short commute is nice. If you don't have your own vehicle and are going to rely on public transit to get around, you'll want your apartment to be located less than 1/2 mile (0. 80 km) from a bus stop. The building may provide a private lot for its residents, or may have reserved parking spaces for each individual apartment. If you're not certain, ask the building manager.

Figure out which amenities you would like to have, and choose a building accordingly. For example, you may feel that an in-apartment washing machine is mandatory, but an on-site gym isn't something you need. Ask the property manager if the building offers perks like: laundry machines in the rooms (or on-site laundry facilities), on-site weight room or gym, pool or sauna and event space.

Find out what else is in the neighborhood with the apartment building. Take a 30-minute walk around the area and find out the distance to the nearest park, whether a grocery store is within walking distance, and how far you'll have to travel for a good cup of coffee or a hamburger.

Taking noise and safety into account. Walk around both outside and inside the apartment building and see if there are any prospective sources of loud noises that could keep you from resting when you're home.

Contact landlord or management company. Before moving in your belongings, you should inspect apartments, and prepare questions to ask. You don't want to be held responsible for damages or taken by surprise if something doesn't work the day you move. If you can, you better check every spot of the apartment to save yourself some trouble and you don't have to take up responsibilities when moving out one day, such as the nail holes in the wall and cracking floor or tiles, to name just a few.

What you need to sign a lease

Passport a / o visa (F-1)

Credit card: Master Card or Visa Card

Bank statement for the past three or four months

Statement of employment and income (usu. scholarship)

I-20 or DS-2019

Tips

First and foremost, do not sign a lease without seeing the apartment first. Do not sign a lease unless you have fully read and understood it. Your lease defines what you can and cannot do while living in your apartment. Violating the terms can lead to serious consequences. Never pay rent in cash! Pay by check or money order and keep receipts of all payments. Obtain a copy of your lease after you sign it.

Ask your landlord some questions, for example, who should I contact if there is a problem? Are there special rules or additional charges? (If so, get them in writing!) Is there anything I can't have in the apartment? Never feel embarrassed to ask as many questions as you have.

You are obliged to inform the landlord or the leasing company 30 days in advance if you plan to move out, and you should find a tenant to take over the lease until it terminates.

Upfront costs of renting

Realtor or broker fee: Typically between the price of one month's rent and 15% of the annual rent.

Application fee: Usually $30-100 per person, covers the cost of the landlord to run your application and background check, credit check and previous rental history check to approve you as a tenant, non-refundable whether you are approved for the apartment or not.

Security deposit: The money you pay upfront to cover any damage caused to the property or unpaid rent, returnable and deductable when moving out. For instance, if the carpet needs to be replaced or there is damage to the walls, these costs will be deducted from the deposit.

First and last month's rent: Your landlord might require an added deposit equal to two months' rent, known as "first and last month." This covers your landlord in case you skip town without paying rent you're contractually bound to pay by your lease.

Renter's insurance: Protect you and your belongings if the unexpected happens. A landlord's insurance policy covers the building, but not your personal things.

Check in

After you sign the lease agreement and get the paperwork done, leasing agency will contact you for your check-in and the exact location of the agency. Remember the leasing agency is not open for 24 hours, so you'd better figure out its opening hours, when your flight arrives and the time you spend on the way to the agency. Some leasing agencies offer late check-in service, leaving you an envelop with a key to the apartment in it, so you can move in and finish the check-in later.

(Adapted from *wikihow.com*)

B2. Words and Expressions

Vocabulary

1. condominium /ˌkɑːndəˈmɪniəm/ *n.* 公寓楼或住宅楼
2. duplex /ˈduːpleks/ *n.* 连栋式的两栋住宅,联式房屋
3. realtor /ˈriəltər/ *n.* 房地产代理
4. wardrobe /ˈwɔːrdroʊb/ *n.* 衣橱,衣柜

Housing Options	**住宿选择**
house	独立住宅
condominium / condo	公寓楼或住宅楼
studios and lofts	工作室和阁楼
duplex	连栋式的两栋住宅,联式房屋
townhouse / townhome	联排住宅
mobile home	活动住宅
doorman / concierge	门卫,看门人
see the apartment in person	亲自去看公寓
do a quick walk-through	快速浏览一遍
live up to one's standards	达到某人的标准
floor plans	楼层平面图
walk-in closet	步入式衣帽间
built-in wardrobe	内嵌式衣柜
pet-friendly	欢迎宠物的

handicap accessible	(残疾人可用的)无障碍的
off-street parking	街边可停车
take public transportation	乘坐公共交通

Vocabulary

1. saddle /ˈsædəl/ *v.* 使承担;给(马)装鞍
2. deposit /dɪˈpɑːzɪt/ *n.* 预付款,押金,定金,存款
3. swindle /ˈswɪndəl/ *v.* 诈骗,骗取(钱财)

Lease Agreement	**租房合约**
apartment listings	公寓信息
apartment hunting	寻找公寓
read the classifieds	看分类广告
ask around	四处打听
reach out to neighbors	联系邻居
look for "For Rent" signs	寻找待租标志
check with a realtor	询问房产经纪人
lease from a reputable landlord	从信誉良好的房东处租赁
previous renters	以前的租客
price range	价格区间
within one's budget	在预算范围内
rent it on the spot	当场租下
sign or break a lease	签租约或解除租约
be saddled with fees	负担费用
occupant and tenant	(房屋)使用者和房客
make a security deposit	缴纳保证金
move in	搬入
moving van	搬运卡车
cover one's personal property under insurance	投保个人财产
carry theft insurance	投保盗窃险
Rental houses come in many shapes and sizes.	出租屋有很多不同的类型和面积。
It won't hurt to get professional help.	找专业人士帮忙也无伤大雅。
Move out before the contract is up.	在合同到期前搬出去。
I don't want to be swindled.	我不想被骗。
Don't rush into leasing.	不要急于租赁。

Weigh your option. 权衡一下你的选择。
Read the fine print. 看一下合同中的小字条款(尤指对签署人不利且易被忽略的条款)。

Vocabulary

1. drape /dreɪp/ *n.* (厚布制成的)窗帘,帷幕
2. rug /rʌg/ *n.* 小块地毯,小毯子
3. pendant /ˈpendənt/ *n.* & *adj.* 垂饰,挂件;下垂的

Living Room	**客厅**
drape/ curtain	窗帘
blinds	百叶窗
loveseat	双人沙发
wall unit	组合柜
bookcase	书柜
coffee table	茶几
end table	边桌
magazine holder	杂志筐
throw	靠垫
rug	小块地毯,小毯子
(wall to wall) carpet	整铺地毯
carpeted floor	铺有地毯的地板
hardwood floor	硬木地板
lampshade	灯罩
floor lamp	落地灯
pendant lamp	吊灯,挂灯
armchair	扶手椅

Vocabulary

1. platter /ˈplætə/ *n.* 大浅盘,大平盘
2. faucet /ˈfɑːsət/ *n.* 龙头,阀门(英式说法为 tap)
3. disinfector /ˌdɪsɪnˈfektə/ *n.* 消毒器具,消毒柜
4. extractor /ɪkˈstræktə/ *n.* 萃取机,提取机

Dining Room and Kitchen	餐厅和厨房
dining table and chair	餐桌和餐椅
tablecloth and napkin	桌布和餐巾
side cabinet	餐边柜
china cabinet	瓷器柜
coffee pot	咖啡壶
sugar bowl	糖罐
salt shaker	盐瓶
serving tray	上菜托盘
platter	大浅盘
faucet	水龙头
sink	洗碗槽
dish washer	洗碗机
disinfector	消毒柜
toaster	烤面包机
blender/ mixer	食物搅拌机
food processor	食物料理机
gas stove	燃气灶
range hood	抽油烟机
extractor fan / exhaust fan	排气扇
juice extractor	榨汁机
full kitchen / fully fitted kitchen	(设备齐全的)全装厨房
meal prep for the upcoming week	为下周准备饭食
balance schoolwork with cooking	平衡学业和烹饪

Vocabulary

1. vanity /'vænəti/ *n.* 梳妆台;盥洗盆;虚荣,自负
2. dispenser /dɪ'spensə/ *n.* 分配器,分发装置
3. plunger /'plʌndʒə/ *n.*(疏通管道的)搋子,装有把手的吸盘
4. drain /dreɪn/ *n.* 排水口,下水道

Bathroom and Bedroom	浴室和卧室
hamper	脏衣篮
vanity unit	(带有盥洗盆的)浴室柜
vanity / dresser / dressing table	化妆台,梳妆台

sink	水槽,盥洗盆
soap dish	肥皂盘
soap dispenser	皂液瓶
medicine cabinet	医药柜,收纳柜
toothbrush holder	牙刷架
towel rack	毛巾架
bath towel and hand towel	浴巾和手巾
washcloth / facecloth / face towel	面巾
hair dryer	电吹风
toilet brush	马桶刷
toilet paper	卫生纸
toilet seat	马桶座
shower head	淋浴喷头
bathtub / tub	浴缸
bath mat	浴室脚垫
plunger	(疏通管道用的)搋子
drain	排水口,下水道
headboard	床头板
pillowcase and mattress	枕套和床垫
fitted sheet and dust ruffle	床笠和床裙
bedspread and sheet	床罩和床单
night table / nightstand	床头柜

B3. Situational Conversations

Conversation 1 Looking for an Apartment

Linda is an international student at University of Virginia and she is talking with David, a counselor, about hunting for an apartment off campus.

L: Linda D: David

L: I have some questions regarding how to rent an apartment here. I don' know the town at all.

D: What would you like to know? How about we check out local newspapers and surf some leasing websites first to see what's available there?

L: Awesome!

D: This one sounds good. "**Efficiency** with view of the lake." **Utilities** and parking included. Newly remodeled kitchen. $470. Can you afford that much?

L: No, I guess not. But that's what I want, isn't it? An efficiency. In fact, the biggest problem has to do with money. Money is at the heart of the matter.

D: Well, the rent of an apartment depends on the value of the area where the apartment is located and it also depends on the size of the apartment.

L: How about this one? "Downtown efficiency. **Furnished.** Parking included. $400."?

D: Sometimes it's good; sometimes it's bad. You have to like the furniture. It's still pretty expensive.

L: Yes, but it's downtown. I would like to take a look at this one.

D: Alright. What's the phone number?

L: 256-7797.

D: Got it. What else do you see?

L: This one. "Two female grad students seeking roommate. Must be quiet. Comfortable downtown apartment." Does this mean I have to share a room with them?

D: No. It probably means they have a large apartment. Probably a living room, kitchen and three bedrooms. They need someone for the empty bedroom. It is very common for students to live together in order to split the rent.

L: That sounds alright. That way they can help each other out.

D: That's right. It might be an advantage for you. You are a foreigner, after all. If they're alright roommates, you could learn a lot from them.

L: Got it.

D: Here's the number, 256-4367. Let's call these two and see if we can make appointments to see the apartments.

L: Sounds good to me. I really appreciate your help on this.

D: Don't mention it, Linda. I'm so happy that I can help!

(Adapted from *tingclass.net*)

☞**Notes**

- **efficiency**: A small apartment. Usually it consists of one large room, one small bathroom and a small kitchen, too. So it's good for one person.
- **utilities**: (*Usu. pl.*) a service such as gas or electricity provided for people to use.
- **furnished**: To put furniture and other things into a house or room.

Conversation 2 Signing a Lease Agreement

Mary, an international student, is meeting with John from the property management company for signing a lease agreement.

M: Mary J: John

M: Good morning, John.

J: Good morning, Mary. Come on in.

M: We talked on the phone yesterday about the lease thing.

J: Right. I forgot to ask you, though. How long did you want the place?

M: Six months.

J: Oh, well, that might be a problem. Usually the office only signs one year leases.

M: Well, one year would be fine, too. I'm not planning on leaving the area anytime soon.

J: Well, if it's not a problem. Then here you go.

M: Just let me read it thoroughly.

J: Sure thing. Just take your time.

M: Looks like a standard lease.

J: Yeah, and don't worry about the **security deposit**. Besides normal **wear and tear**, if everything's all right, when you move out, you'll get it back.

M: OK, I see. I already viewed the apartment several days ago, and signed Apartment Condition Report. Also, I took some room-to-room photos.

J: Good for you! By the way, you can hold on to your condition report for a few days after moving in, or write down any new problems that may arise and call the management company to amend the condition report. Be sure to sign and submit it within a week, though.

M: Ok. Great. Just sign and date it here?

J: Yes. Thanks. You can move your stuff in tomorrow.

M: Wonderful. I really appreciate your help.

(Adapted from *hxen. com*)

☞**Notes**

- **security deposit**: It is the money that is given to a landlord, lender, or seller of a home or apartment as proof of intent to move-in and care for the domicile. A security deposit is intended as a measure of security for the recipient, and can also be used to pay for damages or lost property.
- **wear and tear**: The loss, injury, or stress to which something is subjected by or in the course of normal depreciation.

Conversation 3 Making a Call to the Maintenance Office

Aaron is a renter and Don is from the maintenance office of Meyers Property Management Company. Aaron is calling Don to get his apartment problems solved.

A: Aaron D: Don

D: Good afternoon. Meyers Property Management. How can I help?

A: Oh, hello! I'm **ringing** about some problems I'm having with my apartment.

D: Yes, of course. If I can just get a few details first... May I have your name?

A: Aaron Chester.

D: Ok. And the address?

A: 151 N. Craig Street, New Bridge.

D: Could I ask how long is the lease?

A: It's for a year.

D: And you moved in on?

A: Last week, on 26th, September.

D: Good. Thanks. Now what's the problems you've found?

A: Well, nothing too severe you know, but a few things that have been building up over a few days.

D: Yes, of course.

A: Well, the first thing is the fridge. The seal on the door is **decayed**, and we have a toddler and need to keep milk cool, so we need to get that done straight away.

D: OK... that's the fridge for immediate attention.

A: And then there's front door lock... it's getting quite annoying. It often jams and we sometimes have to **fiddle** with it for minutes before we can get in the apartment. I'd really like that fixed up right away.

D: That's no problem. Anything else?

A: No, that's it.

D: Well, what we're gonna do now is to get someone over to you as soon as possible. How about tomorrow morning? Does it work for you? Or you tell us your preferred times.

A: Let me see. How about 11:00 AM tomorrow?

D: I'd have to check that with someone. And I'll call you back.

A: OK, I've got that.

D: Great. By the way, you can also log onto meyersmanagement. com. Sign up for your online maintenance account. All maintenance requests usually go through our website. It's quite time-saving.

A: Great, thank you so much.

D: That's fine. Thanks for calling.

A: Goodbye.

D: Goodbye.

(Adapted from *IELTS Listening Comprehension*)

☞ **Notes**

- **ring**: To make a call.
- **decay**: To undergo decomposition.
- **fiddle**: To make minor manual movements, especially to adjust something.

B4. Picture Knowledge

Pic. 2-2

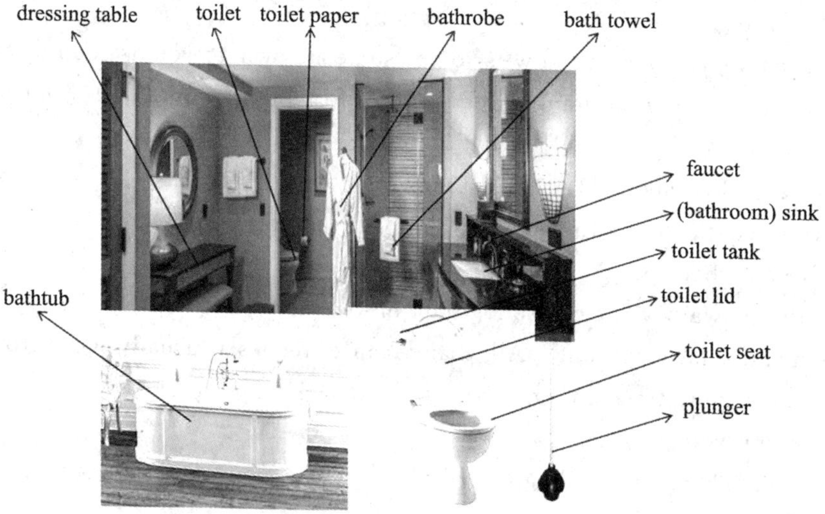

Pic. 2-3

B5. Speaking Activities

Role Play

Design a conversation between an international student and a leasing agent. The student is looking for an apartment off campus. Your conversation should cover the features of the apartment, such as location, facilities and amenities, pet, rent and property management, etc.

You may refer to the expressions below but don't confine yourself to them.

Suggested Expressions:

The apartment is a stone's throw from college.
It's located in a residential setting, two blocks away from college.
It's within walking distance to restaurants, and 1.2 miles from hospital.
What kind of layout you're looking for?
The apartment amenities include private patio and mountain views.
The community has a 24-hour fitness center and a 24-hour billiard room.
All units come with carpeted floors, central heat / air and washer / dryer.
Surveillance system and laundromat are on premises.
Trash removal is included in rent.
High speed internet and cable TV are available.
Are pets allowed?
Do I have the option to renew my lease?
When should I inform the leasing office if I want to sublease my accommodation?
Do you have a deep clean after the previous tenants leave?

Debate

Suppose you have been working for five years. Carry out a team debate on the topic: ***Would you consider renting or buying a home?***

Try to seek diverse perspectives and don't confine yourself to the expressions below.

Suggested Expressions:

Renting a home

It allows you more expendable money in a short term.
You have more flexibility than owning a home.
You cannot make changes to a rented property without the consent of the homeowner.
Renting offers no wealth creation or return on investment.
There is no guarantee that a lease will be renewed when it expires.

Buying a home

It offers the long-term benefits of security, equity and potential growth in personal wealth.

It allows you greater freedom in its use without restrictions often enforced by a landlord.

Being a homeowner can improve your credit profile.

A homeowner runs the risk of not making any profit through resale.

A homeowner has less mobility when it comes to being able to move home.

Discussion

Please conduct a discussion on the topic of "Find a roommate." What should you consider when choosing a roommate for living off campus?

You may refer to the expressions below but don't confine yourself to them.

Basic Discussion

Who will be on the lease (or will all parties)?

Whose name will be on the utility / phone / cable / internet account?

How many people will live in the unit?

How long will each individual remain residents of the unit?

Who will occupy what areas of the apartment?

Does anyone plan to sublet? When?

How will disputes be resolved?

Lifestyle Discussion

What kinds of leisure activities might you want to do in the apartment?

What are your feelings about the use of tobacco, alcohol or other drugs?

What kinds of guidelines should we have for guests and / or significant others?

How will we arrange / organize cleaning responsibilities? How about cooking?

What items and appliances can be shared? What cannot?

What is your typical daily schedule (work, study, sleep, eat)?

What kind of music / TV do you enjoy?

What furniture do you have?

How do we determine internet usage?

Will we have any pets?

Will there be special rules regarding mid-term or final exam time periods?

Financial Discussion

How financially stable are you?

What are your income sources?

How will bill payment be arranged for the deposit, rent, utilities, and other expenses?
What is our monthly deadline for communicating with each other about bills?
How will we track our apartment payments and expenses?

Interpretation

Interpret the following paragraphs into English with what you have learned in Part B.

Paragraph 1

大学生毕业后要做的第一件事情通常是租房。租房有很多注意事项。租客的需求各不相同：有人爱好休闲放松，希望有一个宽敞的客厅，配备组合柜、茶几、双人沙发、落地灯、大电视等；有人爱好烹饪，要求有一个设施齐全的厨房，配备洗碗机、燃气灶、消毒柜和抽油烟机等；有人注重休息环境，渴望有一个温馨的大卧室，配备大衣柜、大床垫及大阳台。出于安全考虑，我们应该先寻找一家房产中介公司并咨询房产经纪人，告知个人预算范围及基本要求。房产经纪人会按照要求帮我们迅速匹配相应的房东和房源。

Paragraph 2

作为租客，我对房子的要求主要在于厨房和洗手间。因为我喜欢做饭，所以我的厨房配备了十分齐全的厨具，比如微波炉、烤炉、榨汁机 、料理机和咖啡机等。这样我就可以经常邀请好友到家里一起做饭和聚餐。这种饮食方式比吃外卖健康，也比去外头聚餐实惠。因为我性格外向，经常有朋友来做客，所以我家有两个洗手间。一个在我的卧室旁边，仅供个人使用，内有大浴缸及梳妆台；另一个在客厅旁边，作为公共洗手间供宾客使用，内有洗手盆、大瓶皂液和充足的擦手纸。我非常注重房间卫生，定期请保洁人员对全屋进行消杀打扫。

B6. Extension

Synonym Discrimination

Can you figure out the differences among the words below?
Group 1：lease / rent
Group 2：condo / apartment / house / duplex / villa / bungalow / cottage / cabin

Extensive Reading

Passage One

Apartment Move-in Condition

Apartment move-in condition is the overall state of an apartment at the transition between leasing from one tenant to another. It is very important to carefully document the state of the dwelling before moving in, since a new tenant may be held liable for any damages that either occurred during their stay or assumed to have occurred during their stay, even if it was a pre-existing condition. If a landlord was unaware of the damage prior to your moving in and assumes that you caused the damage, the cost of repairs (beyond "normal wear and tear") may be deducted from your rental security deposit.

Tips for documenting move-in condition

Don't move anything inside until you have looked over the entire apartment, at least once. Furniture or moving boxes may block problems on the floors or walls.

Go through, room-by-room with a digital camera and a condition report sheet (like the one below). Take photos liberally, of anything that might be relevant. It's likely that your landlord will give you a condition report sheet to return to the rental agency. If your apartment has a balcony, storage area or yard, be sure to check these areas as well.

Turn all faucets / spigots, lights, and appliances on and off; make sure windows and doors lock / unlock; go around with a small lamp and plug it into each socket to make sure each socket receives power. Drapes and window treatments should be relatively clean.

Hold on to your condition report for a few days after moving in, or write down any new problems that may arise and call your landlord to amend the condition report to include additional preexisting damage. Be sure to sign and submit it within a week, though.

Expectations and move-in stories

When you move into a new apartment, your apartment may be in good condition, or not so good condition. Often, some things need fixing. With moving day coming up, it would be useful for people to document the condition of their apartment, both by listing what is right and wrong, and by posting photos of the apartment. This will provide a guide as to what to really expect when you move into a particular apartment, and will encourage apartment managers to ensure that they provide high quality living spaces for their residents (many of whom do not see the apartment before move-in day).

Before Moving in

What to do	When
create and sign roommate agreement	once lease is signed
set up utilities	two-weeks before move-in date
forward mail & display name on mailbox	two-weeks before move-in date
complete apartment condition form	once current tenants move out
confirm when / where / how to pick up keys	two-weeks before move-in date
arrange plans for transporting furniture or belongings	two-weeks before move-in date

When you take possession of your apartment, you must submit an apartment condition report to property management within 72 hours. Otherwise, they will use their own evaluation copy.

Move-in Checklist

Property		Apartment Number		
Area	Good	Fair	Poor	Comments
Living Room				
walls / ceiling				
floor				
couch				
chair(s) / love seat				
Dinning Room				
walls / ceiling				
floor				
Hallways				
walls / ceiling				
floor				
Kitchen				
walls / ceiling				
floor				
counters				
fridge				
range hood				
oven				
Bedroom				
carpet-floors				
fixtures and lights				
doors and locks				
switches and outlets				
Bathroom				
walls (paint / holes)				
floor, carpet				
ceiling (lights, bulbs)				
toilet				
sink, faucet				

Continued

Move-in Checklist				
Property		Apartment Number		
Area	Good	Fair	Poor	Comments
tub & shower				
towel racks				
medicine cabinet				

(Adapted from *localwiki. org*)

Passage Two

How to Sublet?

Many students sublet their accommodations, and this can be a positive and beneficial experience.

What is subletting? Subletting involves a tenant with a fixed-term lease moving out temporarily of the rental unit, and allowing another person to move in for a specific period of time, typically a 4-or 8-month term.

First step

The first thing you need to do when you are considering subletting your accommodation is to inform your landlord of your intentions in writing. It is your responsibility as a tenant to do so.

Next steps

Next, search for a subletter. You can post your place available for rent on the Student Classifieds section. You may also want to post on other websites or ask friends and classmates.

You should introduce all potential subletters to the roommate(s) who will be occupying the accommodation at the same time as your subletter.

It is very important to ensure that everyone is compatible with each other. Once you have found a compatible subletter, you should cancel all bills in your name. This way, you will not be held responsible for any costs incurred by your subletter.

Finally, a copy of the lease agreement currently held between you and your landlord should be attached to the sublet agreement between you and your subletter. It is important that the subletter knows and understands the terms they are agreeing to.

(Adapted from *uwaterloo. ca*)

☞**Notes**

- You become the landlord to your subletter, and will be responsible for his / her actions, i. e. damages, noise complaints, etc.
- You still pay rent to the landlord and the subletter pays rent to you.

Sources of Pictures

Pic. 2-1 Edited and processed by authors
Pic. 2-2 Edited and processed by authors
Pic. 2-3 Edited and processed by authors

References

On-campus Housing. *Ielp*. Retrieved from www. ielp. uw. edu/life-at-the-uw/housing/off-campus-housing/on July 26th, 2020.

Kelci Lynn Lucier. (2018). Getting Along with Your College Roommate(s). *Thought Co*. Retrieved from https://www. thoughtco. com/getting-along-with-college-roommate-tips-793353 on July 26th, 2020.

Allen Grove. (2018). What to Expect from College Meal Plan? *Thought Co*. Retrieved from https://www. thoughtco. com/college-meal-plans-788484 on July 26th, 2020.

Allen Grove. (2019). Reasons You're Required to Live on Campus for Your First Year of College. *Thought Co*. Retrieved from https://www. thoughtco. com/college-residency-requirements-787021# on July 26th, 2020.

Wiki How staff. (2019). Off Campus Housing. *Wiki How*. Retrieved from https://www. wikihow. com/Choose-an-Apartment-Building on July 26th, 2020.

Apartment Move-in Condition. *Local Wiki*. Retrieved from https://localwiki. org/davis/Apartment_Move_In_Condition on July 26th, 2020.

Housing Arrangements. *TOEFL iBT*. Adapted from Rick Crooks &Jiang Pu(2007). *TOEFL iBT*. Beijing: Science Press, pp. 50-51.

Meal Plan. *TOEFL iBT*. Adapted from Rick Crooks &Jiang Pu (2007). *TOEFL iBT*. Beijing: Science Press, pp. 70-71.

Looking for an Apartment. *Ting Class*. Retrieved from http://www. tingclass. net/show-8464-238643-1. html on July 26th, 2020.

Signing a Lease Agreement. *Hxen*. Retrieved from http://duihua. hxen. com/yishizhuxing/3302. html on July 26th, 2020.

Making a Call to the Maintenance Office. *IELTS Listening Comprehension*. Adapted from Hu Min. (2007). *IELTS Listening Comprehension*. Beijing: Higher Education Press, pp. 190-191.

Unit 3 Money Issues

Part A On Campus

A1. Introduction

Going to the Bank

Money is a basic need for everyone and it is especially important for international students. Sources of money come in different forms and can be used for different purposes. Thus, it is crucial to learn how to deal with it before arriving on campus.

Opening a bank account in the UK

If you are going to be in the UK for more than a few months, opening a bank account is a good idea. You can use it to pay bills, make purchases, write cheques and withdraw cash. Above all, it keeps your money safe. You should apply for an account as soon as you arrive because it can take three weeks or more to set up.

When you open your account, you will need to show the bank your passport or national photo ID card, as well as your acceptance letter or introduction from your college or university. You may also need to provide bank statements from your home country account. There may be other requirements, so contact the bank before you arrive in Britain to ensure that you don't leave home without essential information. For more information, you can also contact the British Banker's Association.

Documentation required

- Current passport
- Valid visa (for those from outside the European Union)
- Home bank statement from the past three months

- Proof of address in the UK or abroad (check with your bank)
- Student ID or acceptance letter from your university

Banks in the UK

There are many different banks in Britain. The main ones are HSBC, Barclays Bank, Lloyds Banking Group, NatWest and the Royal Bank of Scotland. Barclays Bank and HSBC both do special international student packages; visit their websites for more information.

You may be able to prevent tax being deducted from your interest. When you open your account, ask your bank for form R105. Remember to let your bank know if you leave the country for a trip; they may think you have left forever and close your account. Also, let the bank know in writing if you change your address.

Currency exchange

Exchanging money into Great British Pounds (GBP) is one of the many little jobs you'll have to do before you arrive in the UK and throughout your stay. It is important to shop around to find the best deals as different exchange rates can have quite a big effect on how much money you have to spend during your studies. Not only do you need spending money during your stay in the UK, but you will also need a transfer service for payment of rent and payment of tuition fees.

(Adapted from *foreignstudents.com*, *savethestudent.org*)

University Scholarship

Studying in the UK as an international student can be expensive when you add up course fees, accommodation costs and living expenses. If you want to study in the UK but do not have enough money to cover the cost of your course, don't worry, there are a number of ways in which you can get help.

Where can I apply for scholarships at UK universities?

Many UK universities have a number of scholarships specifically designed for international students at both undergraduate and postgraduate level. These are generally based on academic merit, but are also often means tested. However, there are usually very few scholarships compared to the number of international students, which means there is very strong competition for them.

Your country may also have student grants or special Career Development Loans which enable you to study internationally. To find out if your country offers these grants and loans it is best to check with your school advisor or careers counsellor in your home country.

There are also a number of national and international organizations that offer international student scholarships to study in the UK. The British Council is the most famous of these, though as shown below, there are other less well-known scholarships too.

How do I apply for scholarships?

To apply for scholarships at specific universities that you are interested in studying at, it is best to look at the finance sections of their websites. You should also speak to the course administrator to see if there are any scholarships specific for your course. You can find more information about the scholarships at the most popular universities for international students in our directory of top UK universities.

To find out how to apply for scholarships from the British Council, contact your local British Council office, as the UK office does not keep application forms. You need to start researching it 18 months before you want to start studying, because the application process begins more than one academic year before the start of the course. Visit the British Council website for more information and to search for scholarships using their scholarship finder on the right-hand side of the website.

(Adapted from *foreignstudents. com*)

A2. Words and Expressions

Vocabulary

1. denomination /dɪˌnɑːmɪˈneɪʃn / *n.* 面额
2. debit /ˈdebɪt/ *n.* 借项
3. withdrawal /wɪðˈdrɔːəl / *n.* 提款,取钱
4. remittance /rɪˈmɪtns / *n.* 汇款
5. transaction /trænˈzækʃn / *n.* 交易

At the Bank	在银行
open / close an account	开户/销户
current account (UK)	活期账户
checking account (US)	活期账户,支票账户
savings account	储蓄账户
certificate of deposit	定期存单
CD term length / maturity dates	定期存单到期日

documentation	必备资料
minimum sum	最低存款额
principal	本金
denomination	(尤指钱的)面值,面额
debit / credit card	借记卡/信用卡
deposit / make a deposit	存款
deposit slip	存款单
withdrawal / make a withdrawal	取款
withdrawal slip	取款单
take out	取出
balance	余额
bank statement	银行账单
billing cycle	账单周期
remittance	汇款金额,汇款
checkbook	支票簿
cash the check	兑现支票
apply for a loan	申请贷款
take out a loan	办理贷款
vault	(银行的)金库,保险库
overdraft	透支
charge	收费
transaction	交易
interest rate	利息
exchange rate	汇率
transfer	汇款
recipient	收款人
Trans Date	交易日期
Your credit card is declined.	信用卡使用被拒。
Your account is frozen.	账户被冻结。

Forms of Payment	**支付方式**
legal tender	法定货币
mint	铸币厂
circulation	流通
cash	现金
one-dollar bill	一美元现钞

one-pound note	一英镑现钞
cheque (UK) /check (US)	支票
signature	签名
check number in top right corner	支票号在右上角
account number in lower left corner	账号在左下角
foreign currency	外币
exchange money	兑换货币
exchange rate	汇率
convert	换算(货币)
expiration date	过期日
security code	安全码
CVC (Card Verification Code)	信用卡验证码
money order	汇票
cashier's check	银行本票
traveler's check	旅行支票
letter of credit	信用证
bounced-check	空头支票

Vocabulary

1. insert /ɪnˈsɜːrt / *v.* 插入
2. receipt /rɪˈsiːt / *n.* 发票,收条
3. application /ˌæplɪˈkeɪʃn / *n.* 申请
4. academic /ˌækəˈdemɪk / *adj.* 学术的
5. counsellor /ˈkaʊnsələr / *n.* 顾问,咨询师
6. tier /tɪr / *n.* 级别

Using an ATM	**使用自动取款机**
teller (US)	出纳
cashier (UK)	出纳
insert the bank card	插入银行卡
PIN (personal identification number)	个人密码
chip	芯片
enter your PIN number	输入密码
select a transaction	选择交易类型

remove your card	取卡
take your transaction slip / receipt	拿走交易凭条

Scholarship	**奖学金**
application	申请
application process	申请流程
scholarship platform	奖学金申请平台
candidate	候选人
align to your interests	符合你的兴趣
academic year	学年
academic merit / performance	学术成绩
transcript	成绩单
academic accomplishment	学术成就
academic excellence	学业优异
key academic strength	主要学术优势
graduate with honors	以优异成绩毕业
leadership abilities	领导能力
student grant	学生助学金
school advisor / career counsellor	学校顾问/职业顾问
tier	级别,(多层、多层次中的)一层
category	类别
award	奖励
cover letter	(申请信)附函
recommendation letter	推荐信
scholarship scam	奖学金欺诈
hardship funds	困难补助

A3. Situational Conversations

Conversation 1 At the Bank

Lisa is an international student at Durham University and has just arrived at Durham. She still carries some cash on her. It is not safe for her to walk around like that. She decides to open a bank account at the bank nearby. A bank staff receives her.

BS: Bank Staff L: Lisa

BS: Good morning, how can I help you?

L: Good morning. I'm a freshman from the Durham University. I'd like to open a bank account and deposit some money.

BS: Please have a seat. Do you have all the documentation with you?

L: What do you need? I have my passport and the acceptance letter from the university with me.

BS: We also require a home bank statement from the past three months and proof of address in the UK.

L: I have the home bank statement, but the proof of address.... Where can I get it?

BS: Are you staying at the student accommodation on campus or a rented place off campus?

L: Student accommodation.

BS: That's easy then. You can go to the housing office and ask for one. Tell them you need it to open a bank account and they'll know what to do.

L: Thanks. I'll be back soon.

(Lisa comes back with the proof of address)

BS: Welcome back! Did you get the proof of address?

L: I certainly did. Here are all the documents you need.

BS: Thanks. I'll make a copy of them. Now, what kind of account would you like to open?

L: I'm an international student, what kind do you recommend?

BS: I can see from the acceptance letter that you will be studying for an undergraduate qualification for at least 2 academic years full-time. This qualifies you for our Student Additions Account for international students. You can pay quickly and securely with a personalized **contactless** debit card and get **cashback** from participating online and high street stores when you shop through us — perfect for busy student life.

L: All right.

BS: Please fill out this form.

(Lisa fills out the form and gets the card.)

BS: Now please set a four-digit password.

L: OK. Do I need to come down here every time I make a transaction?

BS: No. With our online banking system, you can do your day-to-day banking on your mobile.

L: That sounds great! How do I do that?

BS: Just download a free banking app on your mobile. To log on, enter your account number and password. Then you can see the account details and make transactions.

L: That's handy. Thanks!

☞**Notes**

- **contactless**: It is a fast, easy and secure way to pay, for purchases under a certain amount of money (the amount differs with banks). There is a contactless symbol to show if you can make contactless payments.
- **cashback**: It is a service offered to retail customers whereby an amount is added to the total purchase price of a transaction paid by debit card and the customer receives that amount in cash along with the purchase. In this conversation, cashback means a reward program offered by some banks. When you make purchase with a debit or credit card issued by them in certain stores, a percentage of the amount spent is paid back to the card holder.

Conversation 2 Seeking a Letter of Recommendation for Scholarship

Alice is a junior at university. Recently she's been trying to apply for a scholarship. A letter of recommendation is required. So she asks Sharon, a professor in her department to write one for her.

S: Sharon A: Alice

S: How can I help you today, Alice?

A: Well, I came to talk to you because I want to apply for a scholarship.

S: Oh, good. You're an excellent student. I'd be very willing to help you with that.

A: Thanks. I really appreciate it. In fact, I do need a letter of recommendation for this scholarship.

S: What kind of scholarship is it?

A: It's an undergraduate scholarship offered by the American Minority Students Scholarship Association. I'm eligible for it because I'm Asian American.

S: Fine. I know about that scholarship. You have to be a junior, and you have to have a grade point average of 3.7 or higher.

A: I'm a junior now, and my GPA is 3.92.

S: Excellent. So you'll have a good chance of getting it.

A: Well, I hope so. The competition is probably pretty heavy. And they require a writing sample too.

S: Do you have an essay you want to send them?

A: No, they want a special essay. I must write an essay on a particular question they pose.

S: What is the question?

A: They give applicants a topic. The topic is, "The Place of Ethnic Minorities in a Democratic Society." My essay must be three pages typed and double-spaced.

S: That's a pretty short essay.

A: Yes, but I need to finish it by next week.

S: Good luck. I'm sure you will do a good job.

A: I came here today to talk to you because.... Well, I need to ask two favors.

S: Sure. What are they?

A: First, I need a letter of recommendation.

S: I'd be happy to write one for you.

A: And second.... Well, I'm not sure if it's too much.

S: What is it? Do you want me to read your essay?

A: Yes, if you could. I mean, if you could proofread it for me. Or maybe you can give some suggestions.

S: Of course, I could read it. That's no problem. But you need to give it to me soon.

A: I will. I want to write the first draft tonight. So I can send it to your email tomorrow morning.

S: Alright. If I can get it tomorrow morning, I can give you the feedbacks by Friday.

A: That would really help me a lot. I'm very grateful.

S: Don't mention it. I'm always willing to help.

(Adapted from *kekenet.com*)

Conversation 3 Talking about Housing Bills

Gian just moved to the student apartment. She is sharing the apartment with two other students, John and Nick. Today they are sitting together to decide how to split the housing bills.

G: Gian J: John N: Nick

G: Hi guys. Thanks for joining me. How do you think we should deal with our housing bills?

J: I think it's best that we share responsibility for overall household bills. Each one of us manage certain utilities or services. For example, you may take on gas and electricity while I worry about reliable broadband.

N: Good idea.

G: Well, let's see. We have gas and electricity, water and sewage.... I'll manage these two. What other bills do we have?

J: I heard that there is something called student council tax. Since we are all full-time students, we don't have to pay for it, but we must apply for an exemption.

N: I can take care of the application.

J: Great. I think I can help with the broadband and TV license. There is still one more thing, do you think we should get some insurance for our apartment, like the

contents insurance?

G: Good thinking. We definitely need it.

N: I agree. I'll get it done as well.

G: Then it's settled! Each of us is in charge of two bills. At the end of each month, we split the bills and then add each item up to get the total monthly cost for each.

J&N: All right.

> ☞**Note**
>
> - **contents insurance**: Contents insurance helps pay to replace or repair your personal belongings if they're stolen or damaged by a covered peril, such as a fire. So, if your valuables are stolen from your home, or your property is ruined in a fire, you may find that contents insurance helps cover the loss.

A4. Picture Knowledge

1. checkbook
2. check register
3. monthly statement
4. bank book
5. traveler's checks
6. credit card
7. ATM card
8. deposit slip
9. withdrawal slip
10. check
11. money order
12. loan application
13. (bank) vault
14. safe deposit box
15. teller
16. security guard
17. automatic teller (machine)/ ATM
18. bank officer

Pic. 3-1

increase
bank
loan
mortgage
cheque book
fee
counterfeit
banknotes
debt
count
credit card
pocket money
piggy bank
coins
ATM
deposit
decrease
cashier
account
currency

Pic. 3-2

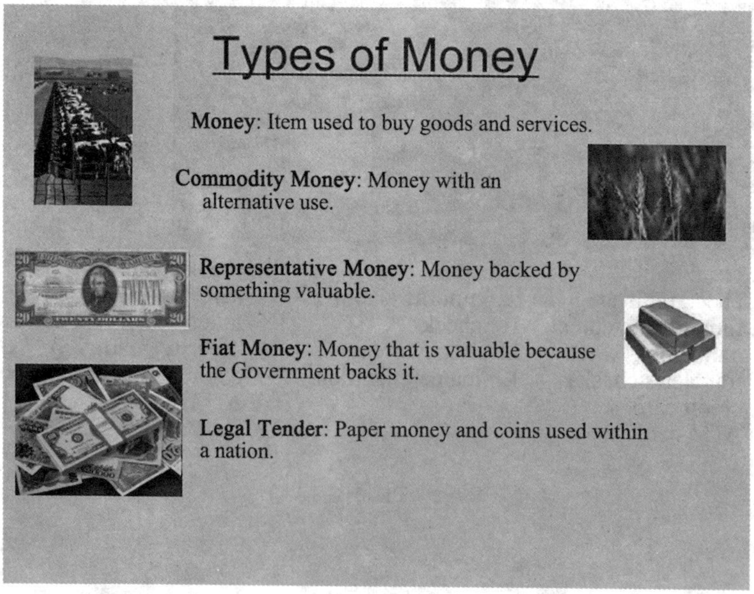
Types of Money
Money: Item used to buy goods and services.
Commodity Money: Money with an alternative use.
Representative Money: Money backed by something valuable.
Fiat Money: Money that is valuable because the Government backs it.
Legal Tender: Paper money and coins used within a nation.

Pic. 3-3

A5. Speaking Activities

Role Play

Design a conversation between a school advisor and a student. The student is asking the advisor for information about scholarship application. Your conversation should cover the type of scholarship you plan to apply for, the qualifications needed, your own achievements and the advisor's suggestions.

You may refer to the expressions below but don't confine yourself to them.

Suggested Expressions:

I wonder if you could help me with this.
What are the individual scholarship eligibility criteria?
You have to meet the language proficiency requirement.
What is your GPA?
Have you won any award or prize in this area?
You need a letter of recommendation from a professor who knows about your academic achievements.
I really appreciate your advice.

Discussion

A recent survey revealed that the average student spends £37 a month on household bills, but it can be much higher for those stuck in overpriced contracts or with fewer housemates to split the cost. The cost also depends on lots of other factors, including where you live, energy demand, insulation, internet requirements, length of showers.... But to give you a rough idea, this table shows the monthly spending of a student on bills, sharing a house with three others:

Average Student Monthly Bills

Utility	Cost
electricity	£12.90
gas	£11.70
water & sewerage	£8.40
broadband	£4.50
TV licence	£3.00
contents insurance	£6.00

Pic. 3-4

Questions to Discuss:

1. Do you think you can afford a monthly bill like that as an international student?
2. Aside from housing bills, what else do students usually spend their money on?
3. Make some suggestions on how to save money on a student budget.

Presentation

Based on three questions above, please prepare a presentation on the topic of ***How to Budget at University***. Choose from the suggested outline below for ideas, but remember to elaborate on each aspect by giving more details or examples.

You may refer to the expressions below but don't confine yourself to them.

Suggested Outline:

- Spend your money on the stuff you need first, and save the "wants" for special occasions.
- Try to cut out the unnecessary everyday spending that eats into your finances.
- Make sure you're getting all the Student Finance that you're entitled to.
- Give yourself a set allowance for each of your spending areas.
- Track daily spending.
- Always siphon off some of your income to a savings account.
- Recycle everything.
- Switch to a cheaper supplier.
- Open a second bank account to set aside any lump sums you receive.
- Plan ahead as much as possible.
- Keep an eye out for deals and discounts.
- Be your own person. Stick to your own budget and stop comparing.

(Adapted from *savethestudent.org*)

Interpretation

Interpret the following paragraphs into English with what you have learned in Part A.

Paragraph 1

到达学校的第一天,John 到宿舍放下行李,拿上现金去采购了一些必需品。他发现,除了平时的零花钱,剩下的钱需要存入银行才比较安全。于是,他向舍友打听了附近银行的地址,然后就带着刚办理的学生卡、护照和现金去办理开户了。到了银行,才得知银行办理业务都需要提前预约。幸运的是,银行经理正好有空。她告诉 John,开户所需资料除了学生卡和护照,还需要学校开具的住址证明、家乡银行开具的的三个月银行对账单。

Paragraph 2

办理好银行借记卡后，Kevin 的生活方便了很多。他去超市购物只需携带一张卡片，再也不用担心现金丢失了。而且，如果需要使用小面额钞票，他可以在超市收银处要求“现金返还”，直接从银行卡里取出 5 元或 10 元钞票，非常便捷。超市还设有汇票办理处，可以邮寄汇票用来支付一些外地提供的服务费用，比如旅行社行程预订。

Paragraph 3

在英国上大学，学费通常比较昂贵。很多学生都希望能够申请到奖学金，来缓解资金压力。大部分奖学金申请竞争都很激烈，对申请人的平均学分绩点要求很高。当然，如果家庭条件不好，也可以申请困难补助。这种补助对成绩没有要求，只需要对学生的家庭经济状况进行审核，符合补助条件就可以获得。

A6. Extension

Synonym Discrimination

Can you figure out the differences among the words below?

Group 1: grant / scholarship / fellowship

Group 2: personal check / cashier's check / money order / traveler's check

Extensive Reading

Writing a Strong Application Letter for Scholarship (with a Sample)

There are many companies and organizations that donate scholarships each year to college students. To apply for this money from school, an application letter needs to be sent. The purpose of this letter is to convince the powers who they should award the money to.

The content of this letter should be centered on academic accomplishments and stress leadership abilities and initiative. This letter must be correctly formatted with proper spelling and grammar. Any errors could be the cause for an immediate rejection of the request.

Before writing anything, make sure to gather specifics that will be needed for the letter. Some scholarships have specific applications requirements and if these guidelines are not followed, the application can be instantly rejected.

Because of the importance of this letter, create an initial draft and look for any errors. The letter should begin with an introductory statement and the paragraphs following should also address the detailed reasons why this scholarship should be awarded.

First paragraph

The first paragraph should talk and focus on the educational and career goals of the applicant. It is appropriate to discuss interests and the chosen field of study. Give them all the reasons they want as for why they should invest in helping this person to further his or her education.

It is always great to show a bit of passion in the area of course work. Organizations want to give their money to a student that is considered to be worthy, not give their money to someone who is going to drop out a few months later.

Second paragraph

The second paragraph needs to focus on strengths. If there are any extracurricular activities or if this person has done any community work, it should be stated here. Any academic awards also need to be listed in this paragraph. If a person was valedictorian or graduated with honors, be sure to highlight this in the second paragraph.

This paragraph is all about selling the person and his or her abilities a bit. Think that extracurricular stuff doesn't matter, think again? The more a person is involved in school and the extra activities, the likelihood of them staying increases.

Never act desperate for money

A third paragraph targets at why this person needs to be considered for the application. This should be spoken directly to the person / company that is handling out the money. It is necessary to be professional, but always be direct. Never act desperate for money, rather desperate for education and the money will help fund this. It is acceptable to talk about housing, books, food and all the costs associated with college.

There may be room for a fourth paragraph, depending on how much a person has to write. Make the reviewer feel confident that the application they are looking at is a sure thing. Highlight any talents and let them feel some confidence that the program will be completed. Since this will probably be the closing paragraph, be sure to restate the goals including both career and educational.

The letter should be around 1-2 pages and never go over the two-page mark. Make the font 12 and use double spacing to make it easy to read. Always use resume or appropriate stationery paper so that it stands out from other letters. Check and recheck for clerical errors and make sure the letter is perfect.

Note: If the letter is being sent via Email, the subject line should have your full name followed by Application for [NAME of SCHOLARSHIP]. The body may be shorter than a hard copy with just the facts. End the email with best regards, your first and last name and your phone number.

Sample application letter for a scholarship

Here is a sample application letter for a scholarship. Any documents enclosed with the letter should be copies. No original documents should be sent. The letter may be included with a scholarship application form or may be sent separately to the scholarship selection committee head.

If it is sent separately, it should be sent by certified mail with a return receipt requested, so the candidate is sure the letter was received. If the candidate does not know the name of the selection committee head, he or she should find out and address the letter to that person.

Name of Applicant
Address of Applicant
City, State, Zip Code
DATE
Name of Head of Scholarship Committee
Name of Scholarship or Institution
Address of Institution
City, State, Zip Code

Cover Letter for [Name of Scholarship] Application

Dear [Name of Head of Scholarship Committee]:
I am submitting this application for the [Name of Scholarship] to further my education in environmental studies. I have studied for two years in [Name of University] and require financial assistance to complete my degree in Environmental Science. I have worked part-time in a recycling center for the past two years and wish to work in the field of environmental sustainability. However, I need a degree to advance in this field.

I spent the last two years of high school volunteering in a waste management facility in the city and have gained a lot of experience in the field. I won an award for creative management for recycling plastic water bottles. My goal is to work to have an impact on many environmental issues such as solar power, wind power as well as waste management. One of the most profound experiences of my life was a trip I took to see the island of waste in the northern Pacific Ocean.

If I am fortunate enough to receive this scholarship, I will finish my degree to qualify for a job in a company that promotes sustainability in their business ethic. My father died five years ago, and I was able to pay for my first two years at university with the insurance money, but my mother is no longer able to support my university tuition.

Thank you for considering my application. I have enclosed a recommendation letter from my university councilor along with the application form and my transcripts. I hope to hear from you soon. I can be reached at [555-123-4567] or at [Name@email. com].

Sincerely,

Signature of Applicant

Printed Name of Applicant

List of Enclosures

☞ **Note**

- The scholarship committee will be looking at hundreds of such letters, and the ones that clearly state the purpose in a brief but thorough way will be the ones that are remembered. It is also important for the applicant to present him or herself as a good candidate for the scholarship. This means that they have the required initiative and motivation to make good use of the money.

(Adapted from *foreignstudents. com*)

Part B Off Campus

B1. Introduction

Part-time Jobs

Sometimes it is not easy for international students to make ends meet. The extra cash from part-time work lets you cover the cost of living more comfortably, sometimes even leaving a little aside for fun. Students who earn their own money tend to spend it wisely. Part-time jobs are often tough, and hard-earned money can be painful to part with.

When you graduate and plan to stay overseas, you must find a full-time job. It is even more important for you to learn to manage your income and other money matters.

Part-time jobs for students

Students often work part-time during their studies — though working during term-time may be discouraged at some universities. If you do work, make sure your working hours fit with your academic requirements and don't distract from your studies. Income from working part-time should not affect your entitlement to loans and bursaries.

Many universities offer sandwich courses. This involves a placement year or industry program integrated into your course. These can provide great experience and are good for graduate employability. Many placements include a salary, and some may lead to sponsorship during your final year.

Outside of term time there are opportunities for students to earn cash and develop skills for their CV. Several organizations offer placements or internships that can be sponsored and only last for a few weeks. If you are just starting university, — remember in retail, Christmas starts early!

Should I negotiate salary?

Negotiating your salary is hard, but not because the act itself is difficult. If you're proficient enough at your job for somebody to want to hire you, you have all the skills necessary to ask for the compensation you deserve. The real challenge in salary negotiation is overcoming the fear that holds you back. That's why it's so important to understand your personal answer to the question, "Should I negotiate salary?".

Money isn't enough

The truth is, money alone is rarely enough of a motivating factor to get people to negotiate. In fact, only a small number of employees have ever asked for a raise.

Usually, it's because even though money is nice to have, it's not enough of a reason to overcome the fears associated with salary negotiation. A \$5,000 raise sounds awesome, but when you subtract taxes, and break it down into a single paycheck, that's only around \$250 a month. And depending on your financial needs, that may not be enough to move the needle.

Think bigger

So if you really want to make more money, don't focus on a single paycheck. You have to think bigger — think about WHY negotiating your salary and earning your market worth matter to you. There is no right or wrong. Your WHY can manifest itself in a thousand ways. But you have to start with a macro lens and think big.

Let's go back to the example of a \$5,000 raise. If we break it down to a single paycheck, it's not really that much. But if we look at the bigger picture, the value grows. Remember that each salary acts as a benchmark for your future earning potential. According to Fast Company, a 25-year-old who is offered a salary of \$50,000 and negotiates it to \$55,000 will earn \$634,000 more over 20 years.

Six hundred and thirty-four thousand dollars is a lot more than \$250. It's enough to take a sabbatical and travel the world, enough to send your kids to the private school of your choice or pay for their college education, or enough to buy a house in almost every city in the United States. If you focus on the lifetime earning potential of your next salary negotiation, and you have a goal for what to do with that extra money, you're much more likely to actually negotiate.

Think outside the box

But salary negotiation can be about more than just money. When you negotiate for the salary you deserve, you aren't just asking for a bigger paycheck. You are advocating for yourself and showing your employer that you have done the research to understand your worth in the labor market. You are living the idea of pay transparency — that employees and employers should both be able to understand how and why pay is assigned the way it is.

The most meaningful part of salary negotiation is that, ultimately, you are standing up for everybody you work with. When employees negotiate, they don't just force their employer to think about how they are individually paid. They force their employer to reexamine their entire compensation strategy. Every time one person negotiates in a data-driven, non-adversarial manner that results in both parties walking away with a better understanding of pay, that person makes salary negotiation a more normal behavior. And that makes it easier for everybody to earn the salary they deserve.

Many people spent far too many years letting their fear of being seen as confrontational or greedy keep them from earning a fair salary. But once they understood how important it was to talk about salary in a transparent manner, they started acting and as a result, they've increased their earning power.

What's your WHY?

Knowing why you want to negotiate is just as important as knowing how much you should be asking for. So once you've figured out how much you should be paid, spend some time thinking about WHY you want it. And negotiate!

(Adapted from *thecompleteuniversityguide. co. uk*)

B2. Words and Expressions

Vocabulary

1. gross /groʊs/ *adj*. 总的,毛的
2. stub /stʌb/ *n*. 存根,票根
3. bonus /ˈboʊnəs/ *n*. 奖金
4. allowance /əˈlaʊəns/ *n*. 津贴
5. commission /kəˈmɪʃn/ *n*. 佣金
6. stipend /ˈstaɪpend/ *n*. 薪俸

Earnings	**收入**
income	收入
disposable income	可支配收入
wage	(周)工资
gross salary	薪资总额
net salary	净工资
pay rate	工资标准
pay stub	工资存根
piece pay / wage	计件工资
basic pay	基本工资
overtime payment	加班费
bonus	奖金,红利
performance bonus	绩效奖
year-end bonus	年终奖
allowance	津贴,补贴,零花钱

commission	佣金，提成
pay raise	涨工资
pay slip / pay roll	工资单/薪资名单
stipend	定期津贴，薪俸
funds	基金
royalties	（出书所得酬金）版税
extras	额外收入
tax rebate	退税
share / stock	股票
dividend	分红
unemployment benefit / dole money	失业救济金
probation period	试用期
submit an expense account	报销

Vocabulary

1. expenditure /ɪkˈspendɪtʃər / *n.* 花费
2. admission /ədˈmɪʃn / *n.* 门票费
3. toll /toʊl / *n.* 通行费
4. alimony /ˈælɪmoʊni / *n.* （离婚后法院判决一方支付给另一方的）赡养费，抚养费
5. maintenance /ˈmeɪntənəns / *n.* 保养
6. coverage /ˈkʌvərɪdʒ / *n.* （保险）范围
7. premium /ˈpriːmiəm / *n.* 保险费

Living Expense	**生活费用**
expenditure / expense	花费，开支
budget	预算
make ends meet	收支相抵
live beyond one's means	入不敷出
live above / beyond one's limit	入不敷出
admission	入场费，门票费
charge	收费，费用
cost	费用，花费
fare	（车船）费
tip	小费

bill (UK) / check (US)	账单
toll	(道路)通行费
pension	养老金
alimony	(离婚后法院判决一方支付给另一方的)赡养费,抚养费
debt	债
fine	罚金
tax	税
mortgage	按揭贷款
hire purchase (UK) / installment plan (US)	分期付款
insurance policy	保险单
car maintenance	车辆保养
insurer	承保人,保险公司
the insured	被保险人
policy holder	投保人
claim adjuster	(保险)索赔理算人
coverage	(保险)覆盖范围
premium	保险费
social insurance premium	社会保险金
housing provident fund	住房公积金

B3. Situational Conversations

Conversation 1 Negotiating Salary at a Part-time Job

While conducting her full-time job search during a down economy immediately after graduating from college, Jenny took a part time job working at a Staples office supply store to earn some extra spending money. It was there that her older co-worker Steve gave her some interesting career advice.

S: Steve J: Jenny

S: Hi Jenny, do you want to get together Friday night?

J: Hi Steve. Sorry I cannot plan anything. I have to work that night.

S: Oh, that's a **bummer**. What about Sunday then, we can watch football together.

J: There is a fashion show on Sunday and I was asked to help and take photos. Sometimes I'd really like a day off on weekends.

S: You work so hard! Have you ever thought about asking for a pay raise?

J: I don't know... but if I could get some extra money from this job, I'd love it. Do you think it is appropriate for me to do so?

S: Of course! In terms of negotiating salary, the first key is looking at the structure of the job. If it's a retail job, with dozens of employees being hired on a regular basis, then it's going to be more difficult to **stand above the pack**. However, if it's a unique position like yours or you can bring a very specific skill to the job, it's often in your best interest to ask.

J: What you said makes sense. But how should I talk to Susan? Do you have any advice?

S: Well, you can say something like, "I've enjoyed the job so far, since I'll be coming in with a BFA degree in photography and specific experience working with top fashion brands, I'm wondering if you have any flexibility with my salary?"

J: Emm... that's a good opening sentence. What if she says no?

S: Well, for a part time job, there are a lot more things to negotiate, such as which days of the week you'll be working, what hours you'll be in their office, and which projects you'll be working on. Sometimes the company will try to make things up with additional **perks**.

J: What kind of perks are you talking about?

S: You can inquire about meals, public transportation or parking, working from home, additional training, and discounts at gyms or clothes, or memberships.

J: Sounds good. If these perks add up, I can save a lot of money and get more experience.

S: Yes. Pay raise can come in different forms. I'm sure if you ask, she will say yes to some of the perks.

J: Thanks for your advice. I cannot wait to talk to her!

(Adapted from *salary. com*)

☞**Notes**

- **bummer**: Something very annoying, disappointing or not convenient. For example, if you left your key at home, you can say "bummer!" to express how annoyed you feel. If you get a disappointing response from someone, you can also say "what a bummer!" or "that's a bummer!".
- **stand above the pack**: Someone is more noticeable because he / she is much taller or is much more capable of certain skills than others. Another phrase **"stand out in a crowd"** means the same.
- **perk**: An advantage or something extra, such as money or goods, that you are given because of your job. It is informal.

Conversation 2 Negotiating Salary at a Job Interview

Every job interview will culminate in an important conversation — a conversation that will impact you, your wallet and your goals for the future. Yes, we are talking about the conversation with your hiring manager about your salary. As the job interview is coming to an end, Alison is talking to the hiring manager Gabriel about the salary.

G: Gabriel A: Alison

G: Well, now let's talk about the salary range for this position.

A: OK. What kind of salary could someone like me expect at your company?

G: In the first three months, you'll be on probation. The salary range for this period is \$3,500 to \$4,000.

A: Thanks. Do you have any flexibility in that number?

G: I'm sorry, but this offer is already near the limit set for someone with your qualification and experience.

A: I see. Can I get a pay raise after 3 months on the job if I can't start with a higher salary?

G: That's for sure. Usually, when you complete the probation and become a permanent employee, the number will be raised to \$5,500 to \$6,000.

A: That sounds like a good starting place, can we negotiate on the details?

G: Sure. The perks of the job include a company pension scheme and a generous travel allowance.

A: That's sounds great. I'm wondering if you provide extra benefits on housing and transportation.

G: Housing is really a big problem and usually costs a lot. We do have some small flats for rent at a company discount. But they might be a little old and small for you. And there is a shuttle bus from the flats to our company.

A: Excellent. I really don't mind if the flats are old or small. I just need a place to stay.

G: I'm glad you like it. Do you have any other concerns?

A: No, that's all I need to ask.

G: All right. I'll be expecting you on Monday then.

A: Thank you. I really look forward to working here.

8 handy phrases for salary negotiation

Once the salary negotiation — either on the phone or in person — gets started, simply keep the conversation relaxed and have the following handy phrases ready:

1. "What kind of salary could someone like me expect at your company?"

If the employer or hirer isn't willing to tell you the salary that they're offering, simply ask the above to start the ball rolling.

2. "What is the salary range you have allocated for someone in this position?"

During the beginning of a job interview or a meeting with a recruiter, ask this question to get information of their salary offer before you negotiate.

3. "I'll need more information about the job / total benefits / expectations before I can name a number."

In the instance the interviewer presses you for a number without letting you know any information; this is an excellent phrase to use.

4. "Can I get a pay raise after 3 months on the job if I can't start with a higher salary?"

If you meet resistance with the salary, ask if you can shorten the period that it takes for you to come up to a raise. This only takes a few minutes to negotiate. Allow the conversation to go back and forth but don't make more than one offer in a row.

5. "Do you have any flexibility in that number?"

Once the interviewer has named his or her offer, use this phrase for a smooth transition into a negotiation.

6. "I'm a bit disappointed with your offer, can we discuss this further?"

If you wish to negotiate on the initial offer, this is another great phrase to start the conversation.

7. "That sounds like a good starting place, can we negotiate on the details?"

Another tactful phrase to respectfully ask for a higher salary.

8. "Can we get that in writing?"

If a better salary or compensation package is reached, make sure you get the details in writing to formalize the offer.

Remember, if you don't negotiate for a higher salary, you'll never have it. It may take some skills in getting what you want, but that doesn't mean you need to be rude or overly aggressive. Keep the conversation simple and smile while asking for what you want.

(Adapted from *jobstreet.com.sg*)

Conversation 3 Purchasing Car Insurance

Raymond just bought a new car. He is planning to buy the car insurance as soon as possible. His friend recommended an insurance company named Triple A. So after making an appointment on the phone, he went to the local office to have an inquiry with the manager.

R: Raymond M: Manager

M: Hi, welcome to Triple A Insurance.

R: Hello. I'm looking to buy insurance for my car. I made an appointment earlier.

M: Well, you have come to the right place. Please, have a seat.

R: Thanks.

M: My name is Roy. I'm the sales manager in charge of car insurance. I heard that your friend is also our customer and he introduced you?

R: That's right. He said your rate is reasonable.

M: You bet. But first, I need you to fill out this form about your car make, registration number, car plate and so on. Then I can make you a quote.

R: OK.

(Start filling out the form)

R: Here you are. Is there any information missing?

M: Well, I need a copy of your driver's license.

R: I have my driver's license with me, but I didn't copy it.

M: Don't worry, I'll make a copy for you. Now, I'll put the car information into the computer and the system will come up with a quote tailored to your specific needs.

R: That's convenient.

M: Yes. Since your car is brand new, I recommend full coverage.

R: What does full coverage include?

M: It includes liability insurance, uninsured motorist, comprehensive coverage, medical coverage, collision coverage and rental car reimbursement.

R: What does liability cover?

M: Liability insurance is a type of car insurance coverage that's required by law in most states. If you cause a car accident—in other words, if you are liable for the accident—liability coverage helps pay for the other person's expenses. The expenses may include costs for property damage and bodily injury. Don't worry, our company packages bodily injury and property damage limits together.

R: I see. How much is it then?

M: It depends on the liability coverage limits that you require. Any costs that exceed your liability coverage limits are your responsibility—in other words, you'd have to pay them out of your own pocket. That's why it may be a good idea to increase your auto liability limits above the state's minimum requirements by purchasing more coverage.

R: I'm still a bit confused. Could you explain by giving an example?

M: Of course. Consider the following: You are at fault for a crash that injured three people in another car. Your bodily injury liability limit per person is \$50,000 and your bodily injury limit per accident is \$100,000. If Person 1's medical bills total \$40,000, Person 2's cost \$30,000 and Person 3's cost \$25,000, you're likely covered. Each person's bills were under \$50,000 (your bodily injury limit per person), and the total cost of injuries is \$95,000, which is lower than your \$100,000 bodily injury limit for a single accident. But suppose all three people had \$50,000 in medical bills, totaling \$150,000. In that case, your bodily injury liability coverage would pay \$100,000 toward those bills, and you'd likely need to cover the remaining \$50,000 yourself.

R: Oh, that's much clearer. Now I understand. What's the state's minimum requirements for the liability limits?

M: It's $ 20,000 per person.

R: I think I'll go for $ 30,000 per person.

M: OK. Then you can get a package deal with the property damage coverage of $ 50,000. Besides the liability coverage, are you interested in the rest?

R: I'm an experienced driver. So I think I'll pass.

M: All right. That totals $ 50 a month. And that makes you eligible for our free roadside assistance. If something goes wrong on your trip, all you need to do is call them. They offer 24-hour roadside service.

R: That's great. How do I pay for the policy?

M: We accept both debit and credit card. The monthly fee will be automatically charged. If you sign here, the policy will be effective from 12 a. m. tomorrow morning.

R: OK. Thanks a lot.

(Adapted from *allstate. com*)

B4. Picture Knowledge

Pic. 3-5

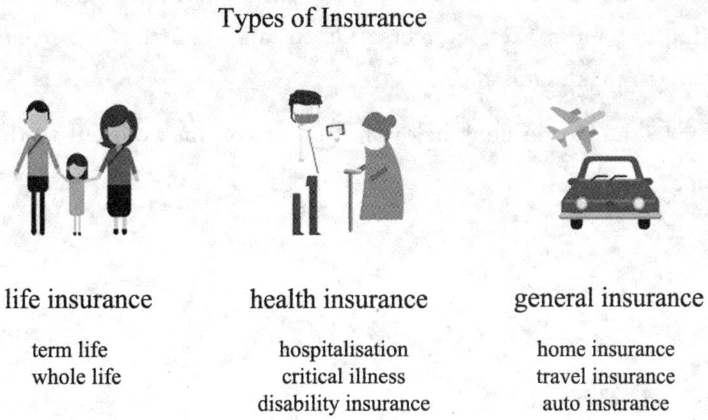

Pic. 3-6

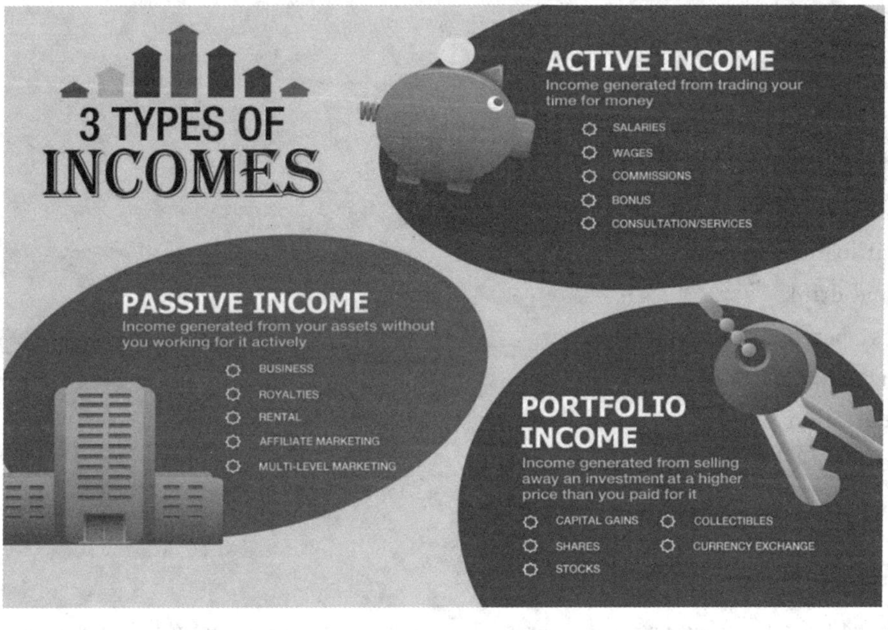

Pic. 3-7

B5. Speaking Activities

Conversation

You and your friend are both new graduates and have just started working. You work as a junior software engineer with a starting salary of \$3,000 per month. Your friend works as an accounting assistant with a starting salary of \$2,800 per month. To save money, you are sharing an apartment. You two feel it necessary to make a list of your monthly income and expenditure and come up with a plan to manage your money. Refer to the following list and make a conversation to talk about how to balance your income and expenditure to make ends meet.

You may refer to the expressions below but don't confine yourself to them.

Possible income

income from work
money from parents
savings
bank overdraft
selling things you don't need

Essential costs

rent or accommodation costs
council tax
utility bills (water, electricity, gas)
mobile phone, internet and TV costs
health insurance and contents insurance

Variable expenses

student loan repayment
food and drink
clothes, personal care and fitness
socializing
transportation
travel
other costs

Role play

You have been working as a salesperson at a foreign trade company for over a year. You are thinking about asking for a pay raise. You did a lot of research and gathered a lot of information on salaries in your field. You also paid attention to the benefits, such as cash bonuses, stock bonuses, and stock price, as well as other types of employer-sponsored benefits and perks like profit sharing, healthcare, and flexible work offerings. Now you are ready to negotiate a salary raise with Robin, head of HR. Robin is an experienced HR manager, and he has been working in this field for over 20 years.

You may refer to the expressions below but don't confine yourself to them.

Suggested Expressions:

In my current role, I'm excited to keep working towards key company goals.

I have tried to grow my personal responsibilities.
Are you satisfied with my performance overall?
As a result, I'd like to discuss my salary.
I'd like to share some of my recent accomplishments.
I've consistently exceeded my sales quota.
I've done some research about the averages for my job title in this area.
Take my tenure here into consideration.
It has been 3 years since my last salary adjustment.
These achievements have made me ready for a raise.
A salary increase of X% is appropriate.
Thank you for your overview.
While I agree that you've made a lot of contribution, a raise of X% is not possible at this time.
I don't have this amount in the budget.
But it's something I could make a case for in the future.
If a pay raise is not possible now, can I get more vacation time or flexible hours instead?

Debate

Nowadays as living expenses increase drastically, many new graduates choose to stay with their parents when they just start working. In this way, they can save the accommodation costs and most of food and drink costs. Parents hold different views towards this phenomenon.

- Some think their children should live an independent life once they start working. They should no longer stay with their parents; they are adults and should be responsible for their own life. With the pressure of life, they are more likely to work harder and get a higher salary.
- The others think that new graduates cannot afford the high expenditure with their starting salary. If parents show support during this critical period of time, they can have less pressure on life and focus more on work. In this way, they can do better at their job and get a higher salary.

Which opinion do you support? Carry out a debate on the topic: ***Parents should not allow young people to live at home again after getting a job.*** Each side should have sufficient supporting materials.

Try to seek diverse perspectives and don't confine yourselves to the expressions below.

Suggested Expressions:

move out	be burdened with
return home	sink or swim

less / more strain on
vital employability skills
live independently
decrease the chance
provide useful support
financial support
relieve oneself of
cheap accommodation
relieve stress
enable sb. to think clearly
sit around
help out
general expenses
rent
physically demanding chores
get by
struggle

Interpretation

Interpret the following paragraphs into English with what you have learned in Part B.

Paragraph 1

Bill 的父母每月都给他一些零花钱，但是他还想额外挣些钱以备不时之需。他课余时间找了一份兼职工作——在图书馆整理图书。这个工作的工资是按小时计算的，比法定最低工资要稍微高一点，他一小时可以拿到 6 美元。每周他需要去三次，每次两个小时。这样，他每周能收入 36 美元，大大增加了他的可支配收入。

Paragraph 2

毕业后，Kate 幸运地找到了一份不错的工作——在一家大公司里做人事助理。在三个月的试用期里，她每个月只能拿到基本工资。试用期满之后，每月的收入增加了绩效奖和一些福利待遇，比如基本医疗保险和退休计划。由于她的工作还需要她经常出入各大人才招聘市场，所以公司还给了她额外待遇——报销来回交通费和差旅费。除此之外，年底还会有年终奖。Kate 对此非常满意。

Paragraph 3

像 Linda 一样在大城市打工的年轻人，每个月都要精打细算地过日子，一不小心就入不敷出。房租占了每月支出的一大部分，而且通常是合租。合租的好处不仅有可以和室友分担房租，还可以一起分担水电费、燃气费、网费等。就算是这样，Linda 每个月的工资也是刚好够花。但 Linda 非常乐观，她认为只要努力工作，将来一定能找到更好的工作，收入也会越来越高。

B6. Extension

Synonym Discrimination

Can you figure out the differences among the words below?
Group 1：allowance / bonus / perk / commission / subsidy / benefit / welfare

Group 2: earnings / income / salary / wage / pay

Extensive Reading

Passage One

Eight Tips for Easy Bills

Here are some top tips on how to sort bills with your housemates and make some big savings.

Put everyone's name on the bills

Make sure that one person is not held solely responsible for an account. It's the best way to get everyone to pay on time as they won't want it to affect their credit score in the long run.

Get your bills sorted ASAP

Get your utilities and bills set up as soon as possible. There's nothing worse than spending the first few weeks of university without internet, and some services such as phone line installation and broadband activation can (annoyingly) take several weeks.

Some companies only offer 12-month contracts as a minimum, so if you set up your account late you may end up paying for months when you've moved out and aren't even using the service.

Always read the small print

Getting stung by surprise installation costs and price hikes can be a real shock, especially when you haven't budgeted for it.

Make sure you know exactly how your contract works and what charges you might be lumped with before signing up to anything.

See if you can get bills included in your rent

If you can come to an agreement with your landlord, it may be cheaper and less hassle to include all bills in the overall figure for your monthly rent payments.

It might be too late at this stage of the game, but it's well worth keeping in mind to ask the next time you're looking for a new place to rent.

Pay your bills on time

Communication with your housemates is essential from the very beginning. Calling a house meeting down the local pub on day one to discuss this stuff over a beer is a great way to sort out how you are going to split the bills without it seeming like a horrible task no one wants to agree to.

Keep the communication going throughout the year and make sure that anyone who makes a late payment knows that they can't do it again, or it will affect everyone involved.

Set up direct debits and standing orders

If you know how much your bill payments will be each month then you could kindly ask everyone to set up a standing order to your bank account. It will save you the hassle of chasing people up every 30 days.

It's also worth noting that paying your energy providers by direct debit could save you a few bucks too by way of a discount.

Split the bills monthly

This is a really important point to stress, especially with bill payments like water which are often taken every three months.

It's best that you take money from your housemates or pay them each month as opposed to just when the bill comes through the letterbox. This will help you to budget and pay in smaller chunks, which is much kinder on the purse strings than being surprised with a bill when you least expect it.

Cancelling your contract

Be aware that there are usually high cancellation costs if you end your contract before the minimum period (typically 12 or 18 months).

At worst, some companies will force you to pay the remainder of the contract in full.

On the other hand, short-term contracts can involve higher monthly pricing or installation fees. So our top tip is to calculate contracts as a full price for the entire year (rather than month by month). This way you can see which will be cheaper overall.

(Adapted from *savethestudent. org*)

Passage Two

Car Insurance

In the US, a car is the most convenient way of transportation. The public transportation services such as subway and bus are shrinking due to the universal use of cars. It is essential for you to own a car in order to get around, which adds car insurance into your daily expenses.

There are generally two types of car insurance policies.

Third Party Insurance: This is the liability only policy cover and it offers cover to any injury / death of the third person caused during the accident of the car. It also offers any damage that is caused to the third person property during the accident. This plan also includes compulsory personal accident cover for the owner-driver of the vehicle.

Comprehensive Insurance Car Policy: The comprehensive insurance car policy covers any loss or damage that is caused to the insured vehicle. It also offers third-party insurance cover and personal damage cover. But, premium amount of this plan is more as compared to the third party insurance policy because it offers wider coverage than the third party insurance.

Premium amount

The premium amount is a very important factor to consider while one buys an insurance policy. It is the amount that one has to pay to the insurance company. Premium amount can be determined by:

City of the customer;

Model, capacity, age, fuel type and other features of the vehicle;

Age and profession of the customer;

Claim record of the customer;

Accessories customization to the vehicle.

Insured value

During the tenure of car insurance, a vehicle is insured for a value that is called the Insured Declared Value (IDV) of the vehicle. It is based on the price of the manufacturer of vehicle minus the depreciation as per the age of the car. There is no limit on the cover for the injury or death that is caused to the third party.

Add-on covers

There are various add-on covers that are offered to the policy holders. These are for the protection of vehicle to ensure for the risks and damage that are not covered under the regular car insurance plans. Add-on features enhance the features of any standard policy but at an extra premium amount. Some examples of add-ons are like zero depreciation, no claim bonus protection, and accidental hospitalization cover.

Insurance claim

An insurance plan with good insurance claim ratio is always preferred by policyholders. There is now a day's cashless facility for the repair of the vehicle at the network garage of the insurance policy. Even if there are no network garages as such, you can take your vehicle to a preferred garage and claim reimbursement for the expense.

(Adapted from *matomeloan. net*)

Sources of Pictures

Pic. 3-1 Retrieved from *easypacelearning. com*

Pic. 3-2 Retrieved from *engworksheets. com*

Pic. 3-3 Retrieved from *slidesharecdn. com*
Pic. 3-4 Retrieved from *savethestudent. org*
Pic. 3-5 Retrieved from *gobear. com*
Pic. 3-6 Retrieved from *secure. fundsupermart. com*
Pic. 3-7 Retrieved from *thumbnails-visually. netdna-ssl. com*

References

Going to the Bank. *Foreign Students*. Retrieved from http://www. foreignstudents. com/money/banking on July 29th, 2020.

Going to the Bank. *Save the Student*. Retrieved from https://www. savethestudent. org/ international-students/top-international-bank-accounts-uk. html#how on July 29th, 2020.

Going to the Bank. *Foreign Students*. Retrieved from http://www. foreignstudents. com/money/currency-exchange on July 29th, 2020.

How to Budget at University. *Save the Student*. Retrieved from https://www. savethestudent. org/money/student-budgeting/student-budgeting. html on July 29th, 2020.

Jake Butler. (2020). Student Bills. *Save the Student*. Retrieved from https://www. savethestudent. org/accommodation/guide-to-student-energy-bills. html on July 29th, 2020.

Scholarship Application. *Sample-resignation-letters*. Retrieved from https://www. sample-resignation-letters. com/writing-a-strong-application-letter-for-scholarship-with-samples. html on July 29th, 2020.

Asking for a Letter of Recommendation for Scholarship. *Kekenet*. Retrieved from http:// www. kekenet. com/menu/201305/238787. shtml on July 29th, 2020.

Negotiating Salary at a Part-time Job. *Salary. com*. Retrieved from https://www. salary. com/chronicles/how-to-negotiate-salary-at-a-part-time-job/ on July 29th, 2020.

Purchasing Car Insurance. *Allstate*. Retrieved from https://www. allstate. com/tr/car-insurance/liability-car-insurance-cover. aspx on July 29th, 2020.

University Scholarship. *Foreign Students*. Retrieved from http://www. foreignstudents. com/universities/scholarships on July 29th, 2020.

Vimonmass. (2014). Salary Negotiation. *JobsDB*. Retrieved from https://th. jobsdb. com/en-th/articles/8-questions-ask-negotiating-salary/on July 29th, 2020.

Unit 4 Shopping

Part A Offline Shopping

A1. Introduction

Why Is Offline Shopping Popular?

With the growing noise in the media about e-commerce and discounts, sometimes we forget that traditional shopping is still the best! Most of the shopping is done offline in physical stores. Here are a few reasons why offline shopping is still supreme.

Happiness

Remember last time you did some shopping and actually felt happy about it. E-commerce is taking the joy out of that experience. Instead of trying the clothes and asking your best buddies how you are looking in it, you check photographs of the dress and how it looks on OTHERS.

You can actually experience the product

While buying offline, you can see and touch the product, personally and physically. You can check how well it fits you and your need. You hardly get that idea by merely looking at images on the computer since you can't experience it and don't know if it meets your expectation.

Personalized recommendation from sales staff

Don't you feel like a princess when the store attendant at the shop drapes the clothes around you and you can actually see how that garment looks on you. It takes a human to understand your specific requirements and show to you exactly the stuff you like!

Satisfy purchase needs immediately

In traditional shopping, if you purchase something, you carry the items as you get out of the shop. Suppose you're planning to go to a surprise party but don't have any dress fit for it. Just head off to a nearby store and buy that special one for the occasion. Online shopping won't save you in such urgent situations.

Reasonable prices

Different from the ever changing prices on e-commerce, there is no such hourly changing discounts in retail stores. In-store customers can rest assured that they are getting the best and reasonable price at the moment.

Easy returns

If you need to ask for a replacement or refund, then just give a visit to the store where things will be processed very quickly. You don't have to wait for days or even weeks to get an exchange or your money back.

(Adapted from *advantagesndisadvantages. com*)

A2. Words and Expressions

Vocabulary

1. rack /ræk/ *n.* 架子
2. ventilator /ˈventɪleɪtər / *n.* 通风口,通风设备
3. kiosk /ˈkiːɑːsk / *n.* 小亭,售货亭
4. sanitizer /ˈsænəˌtaɪzər / *n.* 消毒液
5. infrared /ˌɪnfrəˈred / *adj.* 红外线的
6. thermometer /θərˈmɑːmɪtər / *n.* 温度计

Store Facilities	**商店设施**
elevator	直梯
escalator	扶梯
cash register	收银机
checkout	结账柜台
display rack / showcase	展示架,展示柜
shopping cart / trolley	购物车
safety reminder	安全提示
ventilator	通风口,通风设备
barcode reader	条形码读码器
coin-operated locker	投币储物柜

touchscreen information kiosk	触屏式信息台(亭、站)
baby-care facilities	母婴设施
restroom	卫生间(尤指公共卫生间)
hand sanitizer	杀菌洗手液(免洗)
infrared thermometer	红外线温度计
paper disposables	一次性纸质用品
parking meter	停车计费表
assigned parking spot	指定停车位

Vocabulary

1. bulk /bʌlk/ *n.* 大块,大量
2. spree /spriː/ *n.* 短暂放纵,玩乐
3. impulsive /ɪmˈpʌlsɪv/ *adj.* 冲动的
4. price-conscious /ˈpraɪsˌkɑːnʃəs/ *adj.* 注重价格的
5. trigger /ˈtrɪɡər / *v.* 引发
6. splurge /splɜːrdʒ / *n.* 挥霍
7. dash /dæʃ/ *v.* 飞奔
8. sprint /sprɪnt/ *v.* 冲刺

Shopping Behaviors	**购物行为**
shopaholic	购物狂
shopping addiction	购物瘾
online shopping	网上购物
bulk buying	大批购买
go on a shopping spree	疯狂购物
track the spending	记录开支
establish a budget	制定预算
make adjustments	做出调整
max out the credit card	刷爆信用卡
impulsive shopper	冲动购物者
social shopper	社交型购物者
lone shopper	独自购物者
price-conscious shopper	注重价格的购物者
touchy-feely shopper	果断型购物者
last-minute buyer	最后一刻出手购买者

bargain-hunter	专买便宜货者
first-time buyer	首次购买者
returning customer	回购者,回头客
shop at a less hectic time	非高峰期购物
trigger shopping splurges	引发购物潮(挥霍)
cut back on shopping	削减购物开支
avoid quick purchases	避免仓促消费
keep impulses in check	不要冲动,保持冷静
dash in and sprint back	飞奔进去快速出来
upsell customers	试图说服顾客购买(额外或更贵的产品)

Vocabulary

1. delicatessen /ˌdelɪkəˈtesn/ *n.* 熟食店
2. produce /ˈprɑːduːs / *n.* 农产品
3. generic /dʒəˈnerɪk / *adj.* 普通的,未注册的
4. festive /ˈfestɪv / *adj.* 节日的
5. hamper /ˈhæmpər / *n.* 礼品盒
6. packaged /ˈpækɪdʒd / *adj.* (销售时)包装好的

Groceries	**食品杂货**
retailer	零售商
wholesaler	批发商
beverage / soft drink	饮料
wine and liquid	酒水
delicatessen	熟食店(简称为 deli)
processed meat	加工肉类
fresh produce	新鲜农产品
dairy	奶制品
snack	零食,小吃
condiment	调味品
bestseller	畅销品
home-brand	自有品牌
generic brand	普通品牌
regular price	常规价格
discounted price	折扣价格

festive hamper	节日礼盒
organic foods	有机食品
imported foods	进口食品
bulk foods	散装食品
packaged foods	包装食品
canned foods	罐装食品
frozen foods	冷冻食品
baked goods	烘焙食品
take a sample	取样,试样
check the best-by date	查看最佳赏味期

Vocabulary

1. self-tanning /ˌselfˈtænɪŋ/ *n.* 仿晒，美黑
2. moisturizer /ˈmɔɪstʃəraɪzər / *n.* 保湿霜
3. hydrate /ˈhaɪdreɪt / *v.* 补充水分
4. greasy /ˈgriːsi/ *adj.* 油腻的
5. acne /ˈækni/ *n.* 粉刺，青春痘
6. congested /kənˈdʒestɪd / *adj.* 堵塞的，拥挤的
7. maintenance /ˈmeɪntənəns / *n.* 养护，保养

Beauty Products	**美容产品**
cosmetics	化妆品
haircare products	护发品
skincare products	护肤品
suncare products	防晒品
body care products	身体护理品
self-tanning lotion	仿晒乳,美黑乳
sunblock / sunscreen	防晒霜
shampoo	洗发水
hair conditioner	护发素
face / facial mask	面膜
day / night cream	日霜,晚霜
face / hand cream	面霜,护手霜
moisturizer	保湿霜
cleanser	洗面奶
hydrating lotion	补水乳液

whitening toner	美白紧肤水
anti-aging cream	抗衰老护肤霜
anti-acne cream	抗痘护肤霜
anti-wrinkle cream	祛皱护肤霜
lipstick	口红,唇膏
blush	腮红
mascara	睫毛膏
eyeliner	眼线笔
eyebrow pencil	眉笔
eye shadow	眼影
nail polish	指甲油
foundation	粉底
face powder	擦粉,扑面粉
greasy / oily skin	油性皮肤
acne-prone skin	易长痘皮肤
sensitive skin	敏感性皮肤
congested / clogged skin	毛孔堵塞的皮肤
skin tone	肤色
apply concealer	涂抹遮瑕膏
wear a lot of make-up	化浓妆
put on a little make-up	化淡妆
make-up remover	卸妆水
take off	卸掉
barefaced	素颜的
high / low maintenance	保养得好或不好
A bit goes a long way.	涂抹少许即可。
Give it a go.	尝试一下。

Vocabulary

1. briefs /briːfs/ *n.* 内裤
2. leggings /ˈlegɪŋz/ *n.* 紧身裤
3. hoodie /ˈhʊdi/ *n.* 连帽衫
4. thermal /ˈθɜːrml / *adj.* 热的,热量的
5. premium /ˈpriːmiəm / *adj.* (品质)高级的,优质的
6. unravel /ʌnˈrævl / *v.* (把布、结或线团)解开,拆散
7. hem /hem/ *v.* 缝上褶边

Clothes	**衣服**
shorts	短裤
underwear	内衣
swimwear	泳衣
trench coat	风衣
cotton briefs	棉质内裤
pajamas	睡衣
sportswear	运动衣
pullover	套头衫
leggings / tights	紧身裤,紧身衣
thermal underwear	保暖内衣
hoodie	连帽衫(亦称为 hoody)
fitting room	试衣间
clothes hanger	衣架
premium brand	优质品牌
brand-name clothes	品牌服装
designer clothes	出自知名设计师的服装
vast selection of styles	多样的风格
one-size-fits-all / unisize / free size	均码的
new arrivals	新品
V-neck	V 领
turtleneck	高领
scoop neck	圆领
short-sleeve(d)	短袖的
checked	方格的
solid	纯色的
striped	条纹的
polka-dotted	波点的
It's too plain.	它太普通了。
It's too fancy.	它太时髦了。
It's torn.	它破损了。
It's stained.	它有污渍。
It's unraveling.	它脱线了。
The zipper is broken.	拉链坏了。
It needs to be hemmed.	它需要缝上褶边。

Vocabulary

1. wedge /wedʒ/ *n.* 楔形物，坡跟鞋
2. peep-toe /ˈpiːptoʊ/ *adj.* 露趾的
3. flip-flops /ˈflɪpflɑːps/ *n.* 人字拖鞋
4. bootie /ˈbuːtiː/ *n.* （遮盖脚踝的）短靴
5. pumps /pʌmps/ *n.* 高跟无带女鞋
6. slip-on /slɪpɑːn/ *adj.* 易穿脱的
7. absorbent /əbˈzɔːrbənt/ *adj.* 能吸收的

Shoes	**鞋子**
footwear	鞋类
athletic shoes / trainers / sneakers	运动鞋
high heels	高跟鞋
low heels	低跟鞋
kitten heels	中跟鞋
wedge heels / wedges	坡跟鞋
flats	平底鞋
oxfords	牛津鞋
Mary Jane shoes	玛利珍鞋
peep-toe sandals	露趾凉鞋
slippers	拖鞋
high-tops	高帮鞋
flip-flops / flip flops	人字拖鞋
expensive-looking booties	看上去很贵的短靴
pointed-toe pumps	尖头高跟无带女鞋
slip-on shoes / slip-ons	易穿脱的便鞋
laced shoes	系鞋带的鞋子
lace up one's shoes	系上鞋带
unlace one's shoes	解开鞋带
shoelace and shoe polish	鞋带和鞋油
slip-resistant sole	防滑鞋底
quick-drying vamp	速干鞋面
ultra-light	超轻的
waterproof	防水的
shock-absorbent	减震的

Vocabulary

1. cookware /ˈkʊkwer/ *n.* 炊具
2. cutlery /ˈkʌtləri / *n.* 餐具(刀、叉、勺等)
3. duvet /ˈduːveɪ / *n.* 羽绒被,被子
4. cushion /ˈkʊʃn / *n.* 靠垫
5. accessory /əkˈsesəri / *n.* 装饰品,配饰

Homewares	**家居用品**
cookware set	炊具套装
stainless steel	不锈钢的
non-stick	不粘的
heat-resistant	耐热的
soft-grip handle	软质把手
handcrafted cutlery	手工制造的餐具
silverware	镀银餐具
table linen	餐桌布
bedding	床上用品
duvet / comforter	被子
pillow sham / pillowcase	枕套
sofa cushion	沙发靠垫
bath towel	浴巾
bath robe	浴袍
bath mat	浴室防滑垫
glassware	玻璃制品
matching accessories	配套装饰品

A3. Situational Conversations

Conversation 1 Make Inquiries about Discounts

C: Customer SA: Sales Associate

C: Are there any in-store promotions?

SA: Some are on sales. We've got summer reductions on the moment.

C: Will the membership card give me a discount?

SA: 20% off.

C: May I get 20% off on everything with this card?

SA: Not for new items.

C: What about this coupon? Is there a **catch** when using it?

SA: Yes, for full-priced items only.

C: Where are they?

SA: The two tables over there on the right.

C: Could I use my membership card in conjunction with a coupon?

SA: Sorry, they can't be used on top of each other.

C: If I spend a certain amount of money, can I get some off?

SA: Yes, for every $300 you get $30 back.

C: I see. Does this hoodie have a 50% discount?

SA: Yeah, or buy one get one free.

C: **I'm balling!** What a **steal**! I'll take it! And that pair of black leggings! Do they go with each other?

SA: Black pants go with everything.

C: After everything is totaled, what's the final price? Can I use a credit card?

SA: Sure. After everything is totaled, the final price is $120.

C: May I get a refund or replacement? Just in case.

SA: Yes, within 14 days.

C: I appreciate it!

SA: No problem at all. Welcome back!

(Adapted from *myenglishteacher.eu*)

☞**Notes**

- **catch**: It is a limitation on where and how a coupon can be used.
- **"I'm balling!"**: I am so happy and excited.
- **steal**: It is a product that is obtained at a much lower price than its regular price.

Conversation 2 Shopping for Groceries

T: **Tony** **B**: **Bella** **C**: **Cashier**

Tony and Bella are shopping in a new supermarket.

T: Do you have a coin for the shopping cart?

B: Yes, here you go.

T: Can you believe this place? The selection is **mind-boggling**. Groceries, cosmetics, household items and lots more.

B: This is what you call one-stop shopping. Let's go to the bulk food section first. I want some breakfast cereals.

T: OK. They are in Aisle 3. Let me scoop some out and put a twist tie on the bag.

B: Look! The price of organic brown rice has gone up again.

T: I think the prices are a bit steep.

B: But home-brand products are much cheaper than name-brand products. If we apply for a loyalty card and only buy **generic brands**, we can keep our grocery bill to a minimum.

T: Look! The instant noodles are on special.

B: How much are they?

T: They are half-priced. If you buy six, you get six for free.

B: Then I suggest that we stock up on them. They last forever.

T: Well, check the best-by date, just in case.

B: They won't expire for another 12 months.

T: Woo-hoo! Get 24 packets!

B: The price of canned fruit has been slashed. They are virtually giving it away.

T: Let's get a dozen of cans.

B: **Hold your horses.** These cans are damaged.

T: The dents are tiny. At this price, we can save a fortune.

B: Well, if you insist.

T: We are done.

(At the checkout)

C: It totals $49.99.

T: May I have $20 cash back?

C: Sure.

(Adapted from *easypacelearning.com*)

☞**Notes**

- **mind-boggling**: It is hard to imagine and believe; similar to mind-blowing or incredible.
- **generic brand**: It is a consumer product brand without a widely recognized name or logo because it typically isn't advertised; often known for its trimmed-down packaging, plain labels and lower prices.
- **"Hold your horses."**: It is used to tell someone to stop and consider carefully their decision or opinion about something.

Conversation 3 Shopping for Clothes

C: Customer SA: Sales Associate

C: Excuse me. How much is this blouse?

SA: 24 dollars.

C: Yikes! It's so expensive! That's more than I want to spend.

SA: This blouse won't shrink, wrinkle or fade.

C: Well, in that case, how can I go wrong? What sizes do they come?

SA: Small, medium, large and extra-large.

C: I see. Do they come in other colors?

SA: Yes, navy blue, ivory and violet.

C: I guess I'll take a large in navy blue.

SA: OK. Would you like to try it on?

C: Yes, could you show me where the fitting room is?

SA: If you approach the end of the aisle, you will find it on your left.

(A few minutes later)

C: I am dying to know if I look nice in navy blue. Could you give me some advice?

SA: Sure. You look fantastic! The color makes you look even more smart-looking.

C: Thank you. But I like violet too. I am **debating between** navy blue **and** violet.

SA: Why not take both?

C: Good idea. Could you give me a discount?

SA: That's my best price. You are getting them for a song.

C: Make it 20 dollars and I'll take both.

SA: Let's **split the difference**, say 22 dollars for each?

C: That's the deal.

SA: Would you like them gift-wrapped?

C: No, thanks. They are for me.

SA: This reusable shopping bag is **complimentary**.

C: Thank you. You are so nice!

(Adapted from *english-at-home.com*)

☞**Notes**

- **debating between A and B**: You are hesitating and haven't decided on which one you will choose.
- **split the difference**: It literally means to agree on a price that is midway between the amount being asked for an item, and the amount being offered for that item. To split the difference is a common way to resolve a negotiation effectively, to end a period of bargaining or haggling over a price or fee. For instance, you want to sell it for $120, and I want to buy it for $100. Let's split the difference and close the deal at $110.

Conversation 4 Shopping for Shoes

C: Customer SA: Sales Associate

SA: What can I do for you?

C: May I have this pair of **sneakers** in a size 8 and a half, please?

SA: Sure. Here you go. They are half-priced today.

C: What a hot deal! Can I try them on?

SA: Yes, please.

C: The shoes are too loose for me.

SA: Let me get you a size 8. Try and see how they match you.

C: Er, the front is a little tight and the back is rubbing against my heel.

SA: The shoes will stretch a bit with use.

C: All right. The sole is a bit hard. What's the material?

SA: They are rubber-soled shoes.

C: Are they slip-resistant?

SA: Yeah, and wear-resistant too.

C: What happens if I get them wet?

SA: Don't worry. They are water proof and mainly intended for outdoor sports.

C: I see. They do look very durable. Do they come in other colors?

SA: Chestnut only. It's a classic color.

C: Classic ones always work. By the way, can I get a refund if there is anything wrong with them?

SA: I am sorry you can't. These discounted shoes are **final sale products.**

C: That's a pity. Anyway, I'll take them.

(Adapted from *englishfor2day.com*)

☞**Notes**

- **sneakers**: Light and comfortable shoes with a top made of cloth and a bottom made of rubber; particularly suitable for running and walking.
- **final sale products**: They are normally sold on heavy discounts and all sales are final. Customers are not entitled to a return or refund. They could be overstocked stuff, defective products, or those approaching the best-by date. They could also be the commodities that have been specifically or purposefully selected by the stores.

Conversation 5 Drive a Hard Bargain

C: Customer SA: Sales Associate

C: Excuse me. What's the best price you can give me for the second-hand Mercedes-Benz in your showroom?

SA: That model is extremely popular, so the price is firm — $ 32,000.

C: Even if I were to offer $ 25,000 cash?

SA: Sir, I couldn't consider anything under $ 30,000.

C: What if I were to agree to get it serviced in your garage? Would you **meet me halfway** — at $ 27,500?

SA: Sorry, $ 30,000 is as low as I will go.

C: You drive a hard bargain. I don't want to waste any more time **haggling**. I will give you $ 28,000 cash right now and let's call it a deal.

SA: There's no way I can reduce the price any further, sorry. **Take it or leave it.**

C: Then I am afraid that I have to let it go.

SA: Well, sir. It has been a pleasure. Here is my business card. Give me a call if you change your mind.

(Adapted from *englishwithjo.com*)

☞ **Notes**

- **meet somebody halfway**: You compromise and reluctantly do some of the things that someone wants you to do in order to reach an agreement.
- **haggle**: You attempt to decide on a price or conditions that are acceptable to the person selling the goods and the person buying them, usually by arguing or negotiating.
- **"Take it or leave it."**: It is often used between buyers and sellers in shopping situations where haggling may take place. A buyer may either accept something without any change or refuse it.

Conversation 6 Ask for an Exchange

C: Customer SA: Sales Associate

SA: Good afternoon. How may I help you?

C: Yes, sorry to bother you. I didn't notice there was a grease stain on the shirt.

SA: When did you buy it?

C: The day before yesterday.

SA: May I see your receipt?

C: Yes, here you go.

SA: Do you want to exchange it for a new one or get a full refund?

C: I'd like to exchange it.

SA: OK. Wait a moment, please.

(The sales associate comes back a moment later.)

SA: I'm terribly sorry that these V-neck shirts are out of stock in-store. Would you mind taking one with a scoop neck?

C: I don't think a scoop neck will fit me well.

SA: All right. These V-neck shirts are still available at our online store. Shall I place an order for you now?

C: Thank you so much. Could you get it delivered right to my house tomorrow? The same color, the same size, please.

SA: No problem, ma'am. Please pick a time slot for delivery.

C: From 6 p. m. to 8 p. m. tomorrow evening.

SA: OK, **we are all set.** You may find our return policies for online purchases right on the website.

C: Thanks for your information. By the way, can I wash it by machine?

SA: It's better to wash it by hand or take it to the dry cleaner's. It's preferable to keep it on a hanger.

C: I am so grateful.

SA: My pleasure. We are more than happy to **go the extra mile** to help our customers.

(Adapted from *esl-lab. com*)

☞**Notes**

- **"We're all set."**: It is a common expression that means "we're finished and everything is OK."
- **go the extra mile**: If you go or walk the extra mile to do something, you are making more effort than is expected of you.

A4. Picture Knowledge

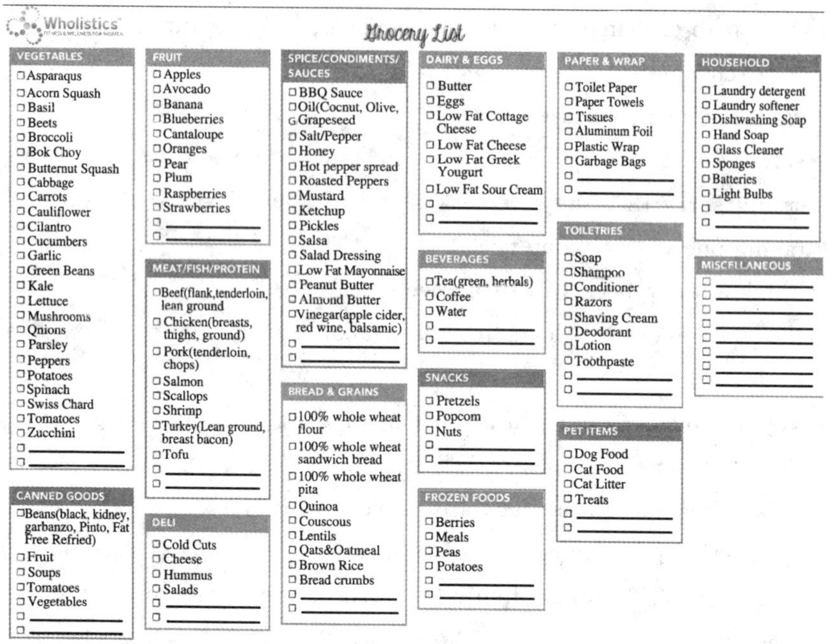

Wholistics

Grocery List

VEGETABLES
- Asparaqus
- Acorn Squash
- Basil
- Beets
- Broccoli
- Bok Choy
- Butternut Squash
- Cabbage
- Carrots
- Cauliflower
- Cilantro
- Cucumbers
- Garlic
- Green Beans
- Kale
- Lettuce
- Mushrooms
- Qnions
- Parsley
- Peppers
- Potatoes
- Spinach
- Swiss Chard
- Tomatoes
- Zucchini

CANNED GOODS
- Beans(black, kidney, garbanzo, Pinto, Fat Free Refried)
- Fruit
- Soups
- Tomatoes
- Vegetables

FRUIT
- Apples
- Avocado
- Banana
- Blueberries
- Cantaloupe
- Oranges
- Pear
- Plum
- Raspberries
- Strawberries

MEAT/FISH/PROTEIN
- Beef(flank,tenderloin, lean ground
- Chicken(breasts, thighs, ground)
- Pork(tenderloin, chops)
- Salmon
- Scallops
- Shrimp
- Turkey(Lean ground, breast bacon)
- Tofu

DELI
- Cold Cuts
- Cheese
- Hummus
- Salads

SPICE/CONDIMENTS/SAUCES
- BBQ Sauce
- Oil(Cocnut, Olive, Grapeseed
- Salt/Pepper
- Honey
- Hot pepper spread
- Roasted Peppers
- Mustard
- Ketchup
- Pickles
- Salsa
- Salad Dressing
- Low Fat Mayonnaise
- Peanut Butter
- Almond Butter
- Vinegar(apple cider, red wine, balsamic)

BREAD & GRAINS
- 100% whole wheat flour
- 100% whole wheat sandwich bread
- 100% whole wheat pita
- Quinoa
- Couscous
- Lentils
- Qats&Oatmeal
- Brown Rice
- Bread crumbs

DAIRY & EGGS
- Butter
- Eggs
- Low Fat Cottage Cheese
- Low Fat Cheese
- Low Fat Greek Yougurt
- Low Fat Sour Cream

BEVERAGES
- Tea(green, herbals)
- Coffee
- Water

SNACKS
- Pretzels
- Popcom
- Nuts

FROZEN FOODS
- Berries
- Meals
- Peas
- Potatoes

PAPER & WRAP
- Toilet Paper
- Paper Towels
- Tissues
- Aluminum Foil
- Plastic Wrap
- Garbage Bags

TOILETRIES
- Soap
- Shampoo
- Conditioner
- Razors
- Shaving Cream
- Deodorant
- Lotion
- Toothpaste

PET ITEMS
- Dog Food
- Cat Food
- Cat Litter
- Treats

HOUSEHOLD
- Laundry detergent
- Laundry softener
- Dishwashing Soap
- Hand Soap
- Glass Cleaner
- Sponges
- Batteries
- Light Bulbs

MISCELLANEOUS

Pic. 4-1

Pic. 4-2

Pic. 4-3

A5. Speaking Activities

Role Play

Design a conversation between a sales associate and a customer in a clothes store. Your conversation may cover inquiries about discounts, sizes and colors of the product, trying it on, complimentary words, payment methods and return policies.

You may refer to the expressions below but don't confine yourself to them.

Suggested Expressions:

- **Sales associate**
  How can I help you? / Are you looking for anything in particular? / Is there anything else I can help you with?

What color / size would you like?
How does it fit? / You'd better try and see how it matches.
The green color really suits you. / This one is more flattering than that one.
There's a discount of 20% on this. / This is discounted by 20%.
Sorry, it's out of stock. / Only XX left in stock.
That comes to... (price), please.
How would you like to pay?
You may ask for a refund within two weeks.

- **Customer**

Would you be so kind to show me the..., please? / I'm trying to find....
Are there any in-store promotions? / Is this on sale? / Can I get a discount with my loyalty card?
Do they come in other sizes or colors? / Do you have this in size 6? / Do you have this in a smaller / larger size? / Do you have this in red?
I'd like to change this for a different color, please.
Can I try this on?
I am debating / torn between... and ....
Can I put one item back? I've changed my mind about this one.
Do you take VISA card? / Do you offer a cash discount?
That's a little over my budget. / That's good value.
I'll take it.

Presentation

Many customers prefer a brick-and-mortar store where they can physically view the product before buying it as well as seeking advice from physical shop assistants. Please give a presentation on the topic: *Your favorite brick-and-mortar store*.

Your presentation may cover the following aspects:

- what and where it is
- how often you visit it
- what you buy from it
- what types of people go there
- why it is your favorite place for shopping

You may refer to the expressions below but don't confine yourself to them.

Suggested Expressions:

outlets
baker's
chain store
street market
flea market
boutique

department store
shopping mall
urban / suburban area
within walking distance
prominent landmark of the area
go on weekly shopping sprees
on a regular basis
shop around
dig through racks
not-to-be-missed deal
most of my basics
trendy items
customized product
well-organized shop
renowned brand
splash out on
loyalty card
people from all age groups
easy returns and refunds
spacious parking lot
free shuttle service
family-friendly facilities
food court
inviting atmosphere
a place for socializing
distinctive shopping experience

Debate

Self checkouts, where a customer rings up their own items, bags them, and pays without a cashier, have been implemented in many chain stores and retailers across the country. Please conduct a team debate on the topic: *Should supermarket cashiers be replaced by self checkouts?* Try to seek diverse perspectives and don't confine yourself to the expressions below.

Suggested Expressions:

implementation
automation
tech-savvy
upsell
marginalize
traditional checkout counters
scan the QR code / barcode
digital literacy
labor cost
job security
time savings
a large influx of customers
average wait time
upfront cost for equipment
take new security measures
adequately trained staff
watch for suspicious activity
anti-shoplifting
thefts and frauds
detect unscanned or switched items
human interaction
customer base
equipment malfunction
software glitch

Write a Letter of Complaint

If you are a dissatisfied customer who would like a refund for defective merchandise, incorrect content delivery or damaged goods, writing a letter of complaint could help resolve the situation. A straightforward letter that clearly outlines the problem and what the company can do to fix the situation is often more effective than simply complaining to customer service. The following sample letter may give you an idea of how to format your letter and what persuasive phrasing you can use to your advantage.

Sample letter

To whom it may concern,

I am writing regarding the lamp I purchased at your store. As a long-term customer of your business, I am usually impressed with your services and the quality of past items. However, upon receiving this particular order, I found the stand of the lamp missing and therefore could not properly set up my lamp. I would like to request a full refund or an exchange for a functioning lamp. Attached is my proof of purchase. I trust that you will respond to this matter promptly. Thank you for your time.

Sincerely,
John Doe

Writing task

You purchased a cellphone, but its touchscreen does not work as promised. You are writing a letter of complaint to ask for a full refund or a replacement.

Writing procedures

- Start with the positive
  I have always been happy with your services and products.
- Express your complaint clearly
  I purchased a cellphone at your store, but its touchscreen is not in working condition.
- Specify important details
  I contacted your customer service on July 5, 2019 .
- Specify what you want
  I am writing to request a full refund or a replacement.
- Establish a time frame for a response
  I expect a response from you within the next 7 working days.
- Give full contact information
  I can be reached at the address given above, or by telephone at XXX-XXX-XXXX.

(Adapted from *wikihow.com*)

Interpretation

Interpret the following paragraphs into English with what you have learned in Part A.

Paragraph 1

导购员：你好，请问需要帮助吗？

顾客：你好，请问这件风衣打几折？还有其他颜色吗？

导购员：虽然是秋季新品，但它打八折，还有象牙白色和紫罗兰色。请问您平时穿多大尺码？

顾客：十二码。我可以试穿紫罗兰色那件吗？

导购员：当然可以。试衣间在走廊尽头您的左手边。

顾客：(试穿后)这件有点太松垮，我想试穿小一码的，白色那件。

导购员：好的，请稍等。

顾客：(试穿后)我拿不定主意该选哪种颜色，两个我都很喜欢。

导购员：那就各买一件吧！这种风衣不缩水、不起皱、不褪色，可谓物美价廉。它们穿在您身上简直完美极了！

顾客：好的，请帮我打包。总共多少钱？可以使用移动支付吗？

导购员：可以，总共 320 美元。打折商品一经售出概不退换，请知悉。

顾客：谢谢告知。

Paragraph 2

我昨天买了一双运动鞋，它是超轻、防滑、速干的，鞋底还有减震功能，我很喜欢它。可是令我惊讶的是，这双鞋竟然是瑕疵品！鞋面有一块硬币大小的污渍，有一根鞋带还是断裂的。于是，我携带购物发票来到商店，要求退货退款。店员却说，这双鞋是打折商品，而且我是叠加使用优惠券和会员卡来购买的，所以只能换货。不过，他们店没有库存了，店员帮我从官方旗舰店网购了一双同款鞋子邮寄到家。

A6. Extension

Synonym Discrimination

Can you figure out the differences among the words below?

Group 1：garment / costume / outfit / gear / clothes / clothing / cloth

Group 2：discount / deal / sale / offer / special / rebate

Extensive Reading

Best Tips for Having a Successful Garage Sale

Ramsey Solutions

If you're looking to make some extra cash or get rid of all that clutter in your garage, there's no time like the present to clean house and turn your unused stuff into a money-making opportunity! But sifting through all your belongings and knowing what to do next can feel pretty overwhelming. That's why we're sharing our tried and true garage sale tips! We'll show you what to do the day of the big garage sale and how to organize, price, and advertise your items.

Tips on how to get your garage sale organized

1. Clean out what you don't need.

This might seem like the most annoying garage sale tip, but it has to be said! Dig through your garage, basement, attic, closets, cabinets, and under all the beds. A good rule of thumb is: If you don't use it or wear it regularly (or you forgot it even existed), it probably needs to go. You'll be able to take inventory of what you have and maybe even gain some extra space in the process. Decluttering never felt so good!

2. Sort and organize your items.

Having a garage sale can be a daunting task, so go ahead and do the major work ahead of time. As you're unearthing all of those tennis rackets, clothes, and old board games, sort them into three basic categories: Keep, Sell and Trash. Don't worry about pricing anything right now—just focus on sorting and getting organized. Your main goal is to get rid of the junk and find a permanent home for the stuff you're going to keep. Once your piles are made, pull out all of the items you sorted to sell.

3. Think about having a neighborhood garage sale.

If you're not too thrilled about the idea of strangers stopping by your front yard (or if you want to split some of the workload), team up with another family on your block or check with your neighborhood association to see if a community sale is coming up.

4. Set a date for your garage sale.

Friday, Saturday and Sunday mornings are usually the best time to hold your garage sale. Here's an insider garage sale tip: consider scheduling it on the first weekend of the month—a lot of paychecks go out at the end of the month, so people will have cash to spend.

5. Get whatever supplies you might need.

You can buy simple pricing stickers and blank labels at the dollar store or any office supply store. Or if you're wanting to be really budget friendly, just pick up a permanent marker and masking tape and get to pricing your items. Grab a table and chairs so you can have a designated area to cash people out (and stay comfortable).

And you're going to need some space to show off all the one-of-a-kind items you're selling. You can set out blankets, boxes and storage containers, or even lay a board over two sturdy boxes.

Tips on how to price garage sale items

1. Name your price.

Be careful not to attach sentimental value to your stuff and overprice it in the process. Do a quick search online to check the current value. Keep it realistic by pricing things a quarter or a third of what they would cost brand new. If you're not sure how to price a garage sale item, here are some pricing suggestions to start you off.

Baby clothes

Suggested price: $1 to $3 for gently used / good condition, or less than $1 for well-worn items.

Adult clothes

Suggested price: $3 to $5 (more if the item still has tags on it).

Books

Suggested price: $1 to $2 for hardcover, or 25 to 50 cents for paperback.

Toys and games

Suggested price: $1 to $3 each.

Furniture

Suggested price: $10 to $30 for low-quality furniture, but no more than one-third of the price for high-quality pieces.

2. Make prices visible.

Make sure your prices are in plain view by using price tags or stickers. Or use colored stickers and hang up a chart that specifies the cost by color, like green stickers are 50 cents, blue stickers are $1, etc. Just try not to confuse your customers. Bigger items call for bigger price tags. Don't make the buyer search for a tiny sticker on that armoire you're selling. Make it big, noticeable and attractive to the buyer.

3. Bundle items.

It's easy to pass up DVDs at $1 a pop. But if you offer them at four for $5, you're sure to catch someone's attention. Look around for ways to make a deal. If it's the end of the day and you really want to move your items, let customers fill up a bag with items for a $5 or $10 flat rate.

4. Don't hike up your prices with the expectation to haggle.

Price your items so they'll sell. Don't set the starting price high and expect your customers to haggle you down. Many potential buyers will walk away from big prices and never even bother to haggle—and you just lost a sale.

How to advertise your garage sale

Don't overthink your garage sale marketing too much. It's a garage sale, after all. But do grab some signs and balloons from the dollar store and draw big arrows letting folks know how to get to your house. Be sure the path is so simple, a first-grader could find it! If you want to advertise in the local paper, church bulletin, or neighborhood Facebook group, go for it.

Tips for the day of the garage sale

1. Know how to negotiate/haggle.

Everyone wants a deal. That's why people wake up early on Saturday mornings to buy your castoffs! If the customer wants to negotiate, then let them negotiate, but stick to your guns if the price gets too low. You're not giving your stuff away! Well, not yet anyway.

2. Make it appealing.

If you really want your stuff to sell, you've got to make it look nice. Before you try to sell those things that have been collecting dust, actually clean them off! Fill bicycle tires and basketballs with air. Scrape the mud out of your kid's old soccer cleats.

If something needs batteries to run, fill it with some half-used batteries so the buyer knows it works. Keep an extension cord handy for buyers to test out appliances that require an outlet. And place a mirror near the clothing and accessories. It might seem silly, but going the extra mile can really make a big difference between making a sale or losing one.

3. Position your stuff.

The morning of the sale, get up early and do a little setting up. Make sure whatever you're selling looks attractive. Put your more interesting items closer to the street so people know you're selling more than just T-shirts, costume jewelry, and old coffee mugs. For everything else, keep it organized, clearly priced, and easy to sort through. Stock your checkout area with plastic grocery bags and newspaper to wrap up fragile items. Those small touches will go a long way!

4. Figure out what to do with unsold items.

If you still have some higher-dollar items left at the end of the day, sell your stuff online! Post something inside your community's Facebook group or list items on *eBay*. Just be sure to always include pictures of your items. People won't even consider buying your antique floor lamp if your listing doesn't have a picture. And research similar items before you price yours so you can get an accurate idea of what to ask.

Enjoy your garage sale profits

It's time to get to work putting these garage sale tips into action. The more you're able to take your time and make sense of your stuff, the easier (and more successful) your garage sale will be. Once you're done, count up all your cash and do a little victory dance. You did it! But before you go depositing all that money into your emergency fund or at your debt snowball, use a small portion to thank your kids, spouse, friends, or whoever helped you out. Pizza all around!

(Adapted from *daveramsey. com*)

Part B Online Shopping

B1. Introduction

Pros and Cons of Online Shopping

Are you tired of driving to the mall and fighting the crowds just to get the things you want and need? Probably yes! The internet has revolutionized the way we shop, making online shopping a massive industry around the world. You can find virtually any product online, as long as you know where to look. With online shopping you can not only save money, but also take the hassle out of traipsing round the shops. Here you can get links to all the biggest and best shops all in one place. However, online shopping may sometimes bring you trouble as pros always come along with cons.

PROS

Convenience

Convenience is the biggest perk. Where else can you comfortably shop at midnight while in your pajamas? Online shops give us the opportunity to shop 24/7.

Better prices

Cheap deals are available online, because products come to you directly from the manufacturer or seller without involving middlemen. Plus, it's easier to compare prices and find a better deal. Many online sites offer discount coupons and rebates.

More variety

You can shop from retailers in other parts of the country, or even the world instead of being limited to your own geography. A far greater selection of colors and sizes than you will find locally are at your disposal.

You can send gifts more easily

Sending gifts to relatives and friends is easy, no matter where they are. All the packaging and shipping is done for you. Oftentimes they'll even gift-wrap it for you!

More control

When we opt for conventional shopping, we tend to end up buying items that aren't exactly what we wanted (but we can't find anything better in the store). Online, you don't have to let the store's inventory dictate what you buy.

Easy price comparisons

Researching products and their prices is so much easier online. We can research firsthand experience, ratings, consumer reviews and product comparisons for most products and retailers.

No crowds

If you are like me, you hate crowds when you're shopping. Being crushed in the crowds of shoppers makes us feel rushed or hurried. Many times, you have to battle for a parking place. All of these problems can be avoided when you shop online.

Discreet purchases are easier

Some things are better done in the privacy of your home. Online shops are best for discreet purchases. This enables us to purchase undergarments and lingerie without embarrassment.

CONS

Negative environmental impact

Having your purchase packed in several layers of plastic and cardboard packaging and delivered right to your front door is good for you, but not so great for the environment.

Shipping problems and delays

Even the best shipping companies and online retailers can't guarantee that you'll get your purchase in time unless you pick it up from a store. Items get lost, detoured, damaged, or delivered to the wrong address more often than you can imagine.

Risk of fraud

If you're shopping online, there's a larger risk of fraud: Credit card scams, phishing, hacking, identity theft, counterfeit products, bogus websites, and other scams are common.

Spending too much time online

Shopping online can turn into a marathon of scrolling and clicking down rabbit holes and before you know it, you've been online for most of the day.

Less human connection

Staying online might be great for a while but sometimes, you might want to go outside, talk to real people, and just be a part of the crowd. A computer monitor can't compete with a real human connection.

Sizes are often imprecise

You can't determine texture, fabric, fit, cut, quality, heft, or durability just by looking at a photo. Products that looked great might feel chintzy, awkward, or cheap when you hold them in your hands.

Returns can be complicated

Some sellers make the process breezy, but many make it extra hard for you to return their product or get a refund. Many times, you can't get reimbursed for any shipping costs.

No sales assistance

If you're confused or have questions, it's just too bad for you. You might have to make blind purchases and mistakes you'll regret later because there was no one to talk to.

No support for local retailers

Many people and places have already experienced the negative and sometimes devastating impacts of e-commerce which take away jobs and devastate local economies.

(Adapted from *thebalance. com*)

B2. Words and Expressions

Vocabulary

1. scroll /skroʊl/ *v.* 滚动,滚屏
2. rate /reɪt/ *v.* 评价,划分等级
3. approval /əˈpruːvl / *n.* 赞成,认可
4. exclusive /ɪkˈskluːsɪv / *n.* 专有,独有
5. auction /ˈɔːkʃn / *n.* 拍卖
6. default /dɪˈfɔːlt / *n.* 默认结果

Web Browsing	**网页浏览**
internet user	因特网用户
default browser	默认浏览器
search it on Google	谷歌搜索
search engine	搜索引擎

scroll bar	滚动条
drop-down menu	下拉菜单
by category	按照种类
back to top	回到顶部
left-click / double-click (on) an icon	左单击/双击图标
open it up in a new window	在新窗口打开
block the website	屏蔽网站
global shopping site	全球购物网站
big-name online retailer	知名网上零售商
buying guide	购物指南
most desired item	最畅销的商品
view ratings and reviews	查看评分和评论
word-of-mouth recommendation	口碑推荐
top-rated seller	评价最高的卖家
100% approval rating	百分百好评
clear browsing history	清除浏览历史
view shopping history	查看购物历史
add to My Favorites	加入收藏夹
personalized recommendation	个性化推荐
online exclusives	网上专卖(品)
auction site	拍卖网站

Vocabulary

1. prompt /prɑːmpt/ *n.* 提示,提白
2. verify /ˈverɪfaɪ/ *v.* 证实,证明
3. check /tʃek/ *v.* 打钩
4. disclose /dɪsˈkloʊz/ *v.* 透露,公开

Create an Online Account	**建立网上账户**
create / open / set up an account	新建账户
follow the prompts	按照提示

access an account	进入账户
close an account	关闭账户
link bank accounts	关联银行账户
verify one's identity	证实身份
register / renew a membership	注册/延期会员
update account information	更新账户信息
enter an active e-mail address	输入有效电子邮箱
type in username and password	输入用户名和密码
reset / confirm password	重置/确认密码
check the box below	在下面方框内打钩
disclose personal information	公开个人信息
in the top right corner of the screen	在屏幕的右上角
log in / on	登录,进入
log out / off	注销,退出

Vocabulary

1. finalize /ˈfaɪnəlaɪz / *v.* (把计划、日期等)最后定下
2. trial /ˈtraɪəl / *n.* 试验,试用
3. installment /ɪnˈstɔːlmənt / *n.* 分期付款
4. receipt /rɪˈsiːt / *n.* 收据

Order and Payment	**订单与支付**
place an order for store pickup	网上购买店内自取
shop a virtual store from home	在家逛网店
add to one's shopping cart	加入购物车
online food ordering	网上订餐
process an order	处理订单
cancel an order	取消订单
finalize and confirm an order	最终确定订单
track an order	追踪订单
repeat purchase	复购

free trial	免费试用
take mobile payment	(卖家)接受移动支付
make mobile payment	(买家)进行移动支付
multiple payment options	多种支付选择
preferred payment method	首选支付方式
make a full payment	付全款
pay on delivery	货到付款
pay in installments	分期付款
secure payment details	保存付款详情
proof of purchase	购物凭证
receipt	收据(亦称为 sales slip)

Vocabulary

1. intact /ɪnˈtækt/ *adj.* 完好无损的
2. carton /ˈkɑːrtn / *n.* 硬纸盒,塑料盒(装食物或饮料)
3. padding /ˈpædɪŋ / *n.* 衬垫,填料
4. package /ˈpækɪdʒ / *v.* 打包,包装,装箱
5. tamper /ˈtæmpər / *v.* 篡改
6. transit /ˈtrænzɪt / *n.* 运输
7. parcel /ˈpɑːrsl / *n.* 包裹,邮包
8. unbox /ˌʌnˈbɔks / *v.* 从箱子中取出
9. perishable /ˈperɪʃəbl / *adj.* 易变质的,易腐烂的

Packaging and Delivery	**包装与运送**
arrive intact	完好无损地送达
carton	硬纸盒,塑料盒(装食物或饮料)
bubble cushioning	气泡垫
gift wrap / gift-wrap	礼品包装
use plenty of padding	使用大量衬垫
thermal packaging	保温(材料)打包
packaged in brown paper	用牛皮纸打包
seal with sticky tape	用胶带密封
attach the label	贴上标签
tamper-evident	防盗启的(关于包装)
sendby express	用快递邮寄

shipping fee / rate	运费
deliveryman / delivery driver	快递员，快递骑手
deliver to the doorsteps	送货上门
schedule the delivery	安排递送
select delivery time windows	选择递送时间段(一般由收货方选择)
drop off / deliver a parcel	送包裹(parcel 亦称为 package)
pick up / collect a parcel	取包裹
parcel (delivery) locker	包裹寄存柜，快递柜
unbox an item	从箱子中取出物品
fragile and high-value item	易碎贵重物品
odd-shaped item	形状不规则物品
oversized package	特大包裹
perishables	易变质食品
handle with care	小心轻放
damaged or lost in transit	运输途中损坏或丢失
free delivery within 5 km	五公里内免费送货
free shipping on orders over $100	100 美元以上订单包邮
at your convenience	在您方便的时候
delivery preference	派送偏好(尤指收货时间)
expect the delivery in 3 days	预计三天到货

Vocabulary

1. initiate /ɪˈnɪʃieɪt / *v.* 开始，发起
2. refund /rɪˈfʌnd / *n.* 退款
3. replacement /rɪˈpleɪsmənt / *n.* 更换
4. hassle /ˈhæsl / *n.* 麻烦，困难
5. faulty /ˈfɔːlti / *adj.* 有缺陷的，有毛病的
6. counterfeit /ˈkaʊntərfɪt / *adj.* 假冒的，伪造的
7. scam /skæm/ *n.* 诈骗，欺诈
8. shady /ˈʃeɪdi / *adj.* 非法的，不诚实的
9. warranty /ˈwɔːrənti / *n.* 保修

Returns and Refunds	**退货与退款**
customer service staff	客服人员
address the problem	解决问题

return policy	退货条款
initiate a refund	发起退款
process a refund	处理退款
request a replacement	要求换货
no-hassle returns and exchanges	轻松退换货
within 14 days of purchase	购买之日起 14 天内
faulty / defective product	瑕疵品
counterfeit product	假冒产品
offer fake discount	提供虚假折扣
not live up to online description	不符合网上描述
scam site	诈骗网站
shady dealing	非法交易
file a complaint	提出投诉
provide evidence	提供证据
present a transaction number	出示交易码
resolve a dispute	解决纠纷
meet / match customer's expectation	满足顾客期望
a product of equal value	同等价值商品
remove the price tag	去除价格标签
in original packaging	原包装
no visible signs of use	没有明显使用痕迹
re-saleable	可再次销售的
non-returnable	不可退的
non-exchangeable	不可换的
be still under warranty	仍在保修期
normal wear and tear	正常损耗

B3. Situational Conversations

Conversation 1 Negative Customer Review

M: Michelle L: Lisa

M: Hey, Lisa. Have you ever had problems buying something online?

L: I once bought a pair of shoes, and after 5 weeks, they still hadn't arrived.

M: Did you get a refund?

L: No, the shoes were bought on a popular shopping website. I gave the seller a bad review. They apologized and begged me to delete my comment.

M: Then what happened?

L: The shoes arrived two days later. You see, a bad review can mess with a seller's reputation, and in turn, their online business.

M: Oh, I see. Do you think the shoes you bought looked as good as they did in the photograph?

L: Honestly speaking, my expectations were not met. I think the seller **misrepresented** his product.

M: Misrepresent?

L: Yes, that's one of the things online retailers often do. They tend to do that by beautifying the pictures on the ads list, exaggerating the performance of their product, or posting false customer reviews online.

M: **Holy cow!** I will never shop online again.

(Adapted from *textrequest.com*)

☞**Notes**

- **misrepresent:** To misrepresent is to describe falsely an idea, opinion, or situation, often in order to get an advantage.
- **Holy cow!:** It is used to show that you think something is so surprising, shocking or impressive.

Conversation 2 Take Precautions

A: Adam C: Cherry

A: Do you think shopping online is safe, Cherry?

C: It's safe as long as you take some basic precautions.

A: Precautions? Like what?

C: Never disclose your password to anybody, and never buy something online using a public computer or a Wi-Fi hotspot.

A: What would happen if I were to be so foolish?

C: Well, there are dishonest people that will try to steal your personal information. They can then commit identity fraud, max out your credit card, and clean out your bank account.

A: Are you kidding? Unbelievable! I just bought a blazer from a **dodgy-looking** website at the mall using a Wi-Fi hotspot. I also told a stranger my password so that he could help me log into my **PayPal** account. I'm such an idiot!

C: Sorry, Adam, but I have to agree.

(Adapted from *forbes.com*)

☞**Notes**

- **dodgy-looking**: If something looks dodgy, it is likely to fail or cause problems. If somebody looks dodgy, he or she is likely to be dishonest or suspicious.
- **PayPal**: PayPal is a leading technology platform company that enables digital and mobile payments on behalf of consumers and merchants worldwide.

Conversation 3 Shop for High-tech Gadgets

J: Jason D: Daddy

Jason is browsing a website for electronic devices.

J: Daddy, **feast your eyes on** all these high-tech gadgets. Cellphones, laptops, camcorders.... They are so cool. Some of them are online exclusives.

D: You are a super fan for electronic devices. Let me buy you something for your birthday.

J: Really? How much can I spend?

D: **I'm not made of money**, so let's say 50 dollars.

J: Thank you so much! I'll buy something that I've been hoping to get for a while.

D: Let me guess what it is. Is it a cell phone cover?

J: Nope. But you are close.

D: Cordless bluetooth earbuds?

J: Not quite.

D: What about a leather case for your tablet?

J: Nah. Do you give up?

D: OK. What will you get?

J: A **selfie** stick. I'll be able to take hundreds of selfies with it.

D: Good idea. Is there any online coupons available for the product you want?

J: Let me see. This search engine will help us with that. Some websites offer coupons for in-store purchases only. Others may require you to buy a certain number of items before you can use them.

D: You have to figure it out before placing the order. By the way, my cellphone is always **out of juice**. Can you order a battery that fits my phone?

J: No problem. Look, there is a big selection for batteries. How about this one? You can expect around 10 hours of battery life with regular use.

D: Great! Add it to your shopping cart!

(Adapted from *englishpage.com*)

☞**Notes**

- **feast your eyes on**: Look at somebody or something with great enjoyment.
- **I'm not made of money**: I'm not that rich. I don't have so much money.
- **selfie**: It is a photograph that you take of yourself, usually with a mobile phone.
- **out of juice**: If your cellphone is out of juice, it is out of battery.

Conversation 4 Return a Product

P: Peter CA: Customer Adviser

Peter starts a conversation over the phone with the customer adviser.

CA: Hello, Help & Customer Service. How can I help you?

P: Hello, this is Peter Gordon speaking. I am calling to request a full refund for the desktop I bought at your online store.

CA: OK. When did you buy it?

P: It was ordered on July 5 and delivered on July 8. The order number is 5570613.

CA: What's the problem with your desktop?

P: I ordered a desktop with a 24-inch monitor, but you delivered one with a 20-inch. And there is a scratch on it!

CA: I'm sorry you are having problems with one of our products. For most items sold at our online store the **return window** is 30 days after delivery.

P: All right. As it was purchased online, do I have to initiate the return online?

CA: Absolutely. Go to the *Online Returns Center* and then click *Return Items*. Just follow the prompts. You should ship it back to the **designated** address to finalize the return. We will be paying your return shipping cost.

P: That's really nice. How long does it take for me to receive my refund?

CA: After the courier has received your item, it can take up to 2 weeks for us to receive and process your return. You can check the payment method that was refunded and the status of your refund in *Your Orders*.

P: Thanks. I appreciate it so much.

CA: It was the least I could do. I apologize to you for any inconvenience that has been caused.

(Adapted from *amazon.com.au*)

☞**Notes**

- **return window**: It is the time span when customers are eligible for a return. If a store has a return window of 30 days, you can return the product for a refund or replacement as long as it's within 30 days of delivery.
- **designated**: If something is designated, it is chosen and set aside for a particular purpose.

B4. Picture Knowledge

Pic. 4-4

Return and Refund Policy Template

Thanks for shopping at My Site (change this).

If you are not entirely satisfied with your purchase,we're here to help.

Returns
You have 30 (change this) calendar days to return an item from the date you receivde it.

To be eligible for a return, your item must be unused and in the same condition that you received it. Your item must be in the original packaging.

Your item needs to have the receipt or proof of purchase.

Refunds
Once we receive your item, we will inspect it and notify you that we have received your returned item.We will immediately notify you on the status of your refund after inspecting the item.

If your return is approved, we will initiate a refund to your credit card (or original method of payment). You will receive the credit within a certain amount of days, depending on your card issuer's policies.

Shipping
You will be responsible for paying for your own shipping costs for returning your item.Shipping costs are non-refundable. If you receive a refund, the cost of return shipping will be deducted from your refund.

Contact Us
If you have any questions on how to return your item to us, contact us.

Pic. 4-5

B5. Speaking Activities

Discussion

Online shopping is convenient and the internet never closes. You can buy whatever you want and buy it whenever you want with just a simple click. Oftentimes, you make unplanned purchases or go over your budget without noticing it. Please conduct a pair discussion on the topic: ***Do people tend to shop compulsively when they shop online ?***

Try to seek diverse perspectives and don't confine yourself to the expressions below.

Suggested Expressions:

overshop (informal)	rational shopper
overspend	compulsive shopper
shop 24 / 7	spend loads of time
entice	ease of payment
cut back on	just a click away
shopping apps	must-have item

nice-to-have item
unneeded item
dazzling ads
tempting offers and specials
scroll through websites
make a hasty decision
max out your credit card
drain your finance
financial wellbeing
resist items on sale
curb online shopping addiction
set a budget with some wiggle room
break a shopping habit
self-regulation

Presentation

Online shopping is a glorious invention which allows people to buy things from the comfort of their homes. But, like everything else, the world of online shopping is not all roses. Numerous shoppers have had bad experiences with multiple shops. Please give a presentation on the topic: ***An unpleasant online shopping experience.***

Your presentation may cover the following aspects:

- what you experienced
- why it happened
- how the problem was addressed
- what you learned from it

You may refer to the expressions below but don't confine yourself to them.

Suggested Expressions:

refundable
counterfeit
defective / faulty
misleading ads
not live up to online description
sell off overstocks
damaged / lost in transit
incorrect product / amount / size
delivery delay
dodgy-looking website
dishonest retailer
negative customer feedback
low credit rating
return restrictions
final sales
bargain hunter
first-time buyer
keep copies of receipts
take precautions
customer loyalty
file a complaint
resolve the issue
responsive and accommodating
pay shipping costs for the replacement
refund a price difference
reship a product
get a full refund
within the promised time frame

Retelling

Read the story below and retell it to the class with details.

Connecticut Shoppers Must Pay Plastic Bag Tax

Casey Leins

Starting Thursday, Connecticut residents will have to pay 10 cents for single-use plastic bags at restaurants and grocery stores. The new law, which goes into effect on Aug. 1, is meant to be a transition before July 2021 when single-use bags will be banned in the state. It does not include bags used for meat and produce or bags used at dry cleaner's. The idea is that shoppers will begin to purchase and use reusable bags, or recycle plastic bags. But some retailers are starting the ban Thursday instead, eliminating plastic bags instead of charging the sales tax.

(Adapted from *usnews. com*)

Interpretation

Interpret the following paragraphs into English with what you have learned in Part B.

Paragraph 1

网购不受地域和时间限制，只需点击一下鼠标，即可实现随时随地全球购，所订购的商品将直接被派送上门。但网购商品通常使用大量衬垫、纸板和塑料来包装，而且运输过程也会对环境产生影响，去实体店购物则不存在这个问题。在实体店，你可以试穿或试用心仪的商品，倾听导购员的讲解和建议，有时还能讨价还价，而且退换货服务也更及时周到。我个人非常享受实体店的购物体验！

Paragraph 2

我舍友是个网购迷。她每天都会花费两三个小时浏览购物网站，看到喜欢的东西就加入购物车，尤其对打折商品毫无抵抗力，是一个典型的冲动型购物者。她几乎每周都会收到快递，包装盒和包装袋堆满了宿舍。因此，她的购物开支一路飙升，信用卡经常透支，个人财务状况堪忧。我建议她卸载手机上的购物 App，每月制定购物预算，并尽力克制网购瘾。她正在试图改变自己不理性的购物习惯。

B6. Extension

Synonym Discrimination

Can you figure out the differences among the words below?

Group 1: product / merchandise / commodity / goods
Group 2: fake / counterfeit / bogus / false / faulty / defective
Group 3: exchange / change / interchange / replace / swap / switch

Extensive Reading

2019 Online Shopping Behavior: What Do Customers Want?

Krystina Morgan

The 2019 Online Shopper Survey carried out by 2Checkout between May and July 2019 has revealed consumer preferences, challenges and behavior when it comes to buying online. The answers gathered from respondents across the world give insights ranging from what products they buy online to what influences their buying decisions or cross-border shopping choices.

Online shopper behavior is something that is constantly being studied to try and improve consumers' overall experience. Even with direct answers to questions such as "What makes shoppers abandon their cart" or "What is the most popular item bought online", every consumer is different and there are no definitive answers. However, the survey results from 2Checkout can help retailers get that much closer to perfecting their e-commerce platform.

More shoppers are buying online for the holidays

Last year, holiday ecommerce sales grew to $126 billion, a 16.5 percent increase from the $108.2 billion generated in 2017. Cyber Monday alone generated $7.9 billion in online sales in 2018, making it the biggest sales day in U.S. e-commerce history. Even though 2019 e-commerce sales are predicting a slower-than-expected growth, there is still an anticipated 9 percent year-over-year growth.

Shopping internationally is also another important factor of buying online that has seen an increase in use over the years. 2Checkout found that 72 percent of shoppers worldwide have bought online from another country in the last year. Some of the most important aspects for buying internationally were being able to find products that weren't available in the shopper's home market (51%), items were cheaper from another country (49%) and free international delivery was offered (31%). International delivery can be pricey for indie retailers, but it's important to know what your customers are looking for.

What are consumers purchasing online

2Checkout reports that more than half of shoppers make online purchases a few times a year (30%) or more seldom (27%). However, 26 percent of respondents say they make purchases once or twice a month, while 17 percent purchase online once a week or more. This means there's still a good amount of consumers shopping online.

What exactly your customers are looking to buy online is another big topic for retailers.

Computers and electronics are the most popular physical goods purchased online, closely followed by clothing and accessories as well as mobile phones and tablets. Since clothing can be difficult to buy online between the right sizing and comfort style, it makes sense that category is not the most sought after online purchase. Offering easy returns or exchanges for consumers can change this and make them a little more willing to buy clothes online.

Make your website just as inviting as your physical storefront

There's a certain comfort factor in being able to see and touch products in person, which is one of the reasons why brick and mortar is still thriving. As indie retailers make their storefront inviting for their customers to shop from, the same should go for the website. Google alone can provide consumers with millions of other websites, so why should they buy from yours?

In a sign of the times, data privacy and security are considered a "very important" decision factor by more than three quarters of shoppers who took the survey from 2Checkout. Good vendor reputation and clear delivery, warranty and refund policies are also essential when it comes to persuading shoppers to buy online.

Abandoned shopping carts

There's also the shopping cart abandonment issue. Your website may look inviting to shop from, but now something has made the customer decide to opt out on their purchase. 2Checkout's survey revealed multiple reasons why consumers abandon shopping carts. 39 percent decided last minute that they did not need the product and 37 percent found unexpected extra fees at checkout. Following closely behind the two main reasons for customers abandoning their cart were insufficient product details (31%), their preferred payment method wasn't accepted (27%) and there was a lengthy delivery time (24%).

In order to make the shopping cart abandonment issues less lengthy, one thing you can do as a business owner is to increase the number of payment options offered. Most survey respondents reported that they use credit and debit cards the most (63%) when making an online purchase, while 39 percent said they use PayPal the most. Offering PayPal as well as more credit card options for consumers can help to reduce the amount of abandoned shopping carts.

Be there for your customers

As intense as the holidays can get for retailers, the single most important thing to be aware of is taking care of customers. Some ways you can accomplish this are by making sure they are being helped on the sales floor, creating a seamless checkout experience both online and in-store and making sure any issues are taken care of. 2Checkout's survey found that a whopping 62 percent of respondents prefer to receive customer support through email. Online chats (29%) and toll-free numbers (35%) are some other major ways to help consumers. All hands on deck this holiday season!

(Adapted from *independentretailer.com*)

Sources of Pictures

Pic. 4-1 Retrieved from *amazon.co.uk*
Pic. 4-2 Retrieved from *engames.eu*
Pic. 4-3 Retrieved from *7esl.com*
Pic. 4-4 Retrieved from *sidebysidereviews.com*
Pic. 4-5 Retrieved from *termsfeed.com*

References

Why is Offline Shopping Popular?. *Advantages N Disadvantages*. Retrieved from https://www.advantagesndisadvantages.com/advantages-disadvantages-offline-shopping.html on July 20th, 2020.

Make Inquiries about Discounts. *My English Teacher*. Retrieved from https://www.myenglishteacher.eu/blog/shopping-vocabulary/#show on July 20th, 2020.

Shopping for Groceries. *Easy Pace Learning*. Retrieved from https://www.easypacelearning.com/all-lessons/english-lessons-level-3/207-supermarket-shopping-english-lesson on July 20th, 2020.

Shopping for Clothes. *english-at-home*. Retrieved from https://www.english-at-home.com/shopping-conversations/on July 20th, 2020.

Shopping for Shoes. *ENGLISH FOR 2 DAY*. Retrieved from https://www.englishfor2day.com/article/dialogue/1162 on July 20th, 2020.

Drive a Hard Bargain. *English With Jo*. Retrieved from http://www.englishwithjo.com/english-conversation-bargaining/on July 20th, 2020.

Ask for an Exchange. *ESL CYBER LISTENING LAB*. Retrieved from https://www.esl-lab.com/difficult/store-returns-script/on July 20th, 2020.

Jaspreet kaur. (2018). Talk about Your Favorite Place for Shopping. *IELTS FEVER*. Retrieved from https://ieltsfever.org/talk-favorite-place-shopping/on July 20th, 2020.

Ben Dwyer. (2019). Self Checkout: Should You Implement It?. *CardFellow*. Retrieved from https://www.cardfellow.com/blog/self-checkout-should-you-implement-it/on July 20th, 2020.

Alice Wu. (2019). Write a Letter of Complaint. *Wikihow*. Retrieved from https://www.wikihow.com/Start-a-Complaint-Letter#References on July 20th, 2020.

Ramsey Solutions. (2020). Best Tips for Having a Successful Garage Sale. *RAMSEY*. Retrieved from https://www.daveramsey.com/blog/garage-sale-tips on July 20th, 2020.

Donna L. Montaldo. (2020). Pros and Cons of Online Shopping. *The Balance*. Retrieved from https://www. https://www.thebalance.com/the-pros-and-cons-of-online-shopping-939775/the-pros-and-cons-of-online-shopping-939775 on July 20th, 2020.

Elise Dopson. (2018). Negative Customer Review. *TEXT REQUEST*. Retrieved from https://www.textrequest.com/blog/negative-customer-reviews/on July 20th, 2020.

Abe Garver. (2012). Take Precautions. *Forbes*. Retrieved from https://www.forbes.com/sites/abegarver/2012/09/11/the-top-five-dangers-of-online-shopping-precautions-to-take/? sh=70d8fce03cf2 on July 20th, 2020.

Shop for High-tech Gadgets. *Just Good English*. Retrieved from https://www.englishpage.com/vocabulary/interactivelesson11a.htm on July 20th, 2020.

Return a Product. *Amazon*. Retrieved from https://www.amazon.com.au/spr/returns/on July 20th, 2020.

Michel Millot. (2018). Buying Cheap. *Researchgate*. Retrieved from https://www.researchgate.net/publication/328265352_Buying_Cheap on July 20th, 2020.

Clinton M. Sandvick. (2020). How to Report a Fraud Website. *Wikihow*. Retrieved from https://www.wikihow.com/Report-a-Fraud-Website on July 20th, 2020.

Casey Leins. (2019). Connecticut Shoppers Must Pay Plastic Bag Tax. *Usnews*. Retrieved from https://www.usnews.com/news/best-states/articles/2019-08-01/connecticut-shoppers must-pay-plastic-bag-tax on July 20th, 2020.

Krystina Morgan. (2019). 2019 Online Shopping Behavior: What do Customers Want? *Independentretailer*. Retrieved from https://independentretailer.com/? s = 2019 + Online+ Shopping + Behavior% 3A + What + Do + Customers + Want% 3F on July 20th, 2020.

Unit 5 Describing Food

Part A Food Taste and Texture

A1. Introduction

A Sensory Approach to Food

Eating and drinking are multi-sensory experiences. It's for this reason restaurateurs would spend a pretty penny to swank up their restaurants. In today's kitchens, chefs are culinary artists who balance color and contrast to make their dishes shine with aesthetic appeal, capitalizing on the fact that we eat first with our eyes, not our mouths.

On the shelves of modern supermarkets, the variety of foods on offer could easily feature in the travelogue of a foodie's pilgrimage around the globe, with prettily-packed produce promising extraordinary pleasures for the palate.

More than just taste

In the world of food, appearances matter. And the factors that contribute to this are varied, involving everything from color changes that may occur during processing to the combination of ingredients used to create the final product.

Smell is another factor that greatly influences food acceptance. Carried by the air to the nose and transmitted by the olfactory nerves to our brain, aroma is one of the first ways we interact with a food item we're about to consume.

This sensory stimulus is so powerful, and it is often used as a marketing tool to entice customers to stick around longer in a store, spend more money or to return again and again.

Scent or aroma marketing is a strategy commonly deployed by coffee shops and bakeries for exactly this purpose. Starbucks, for example, is said to hide the odor of the foods it prepares in-store by adding the scent of coffee to their HVAC systems. The reason? Its customers enjoy the smell of freshly brewed coffee. And secondly, Starbucks is first and foremost a coffeehouse — the smell of scrambled eggs and ham and cheese toasties might take away from that experience.

What is texture

Texture is yet another organoleptic property that could make or break customer experience in food. It refers to our perception or interpretation of food structure when a food item is held in our fingers (think fried chicken), pushed by the tongue against the palate or chewed by the teeth and then sensed within the oral cavity.

To lesser-trained taste buds, this sensory quality isn't always appreciated as a factor that determines what makes a food product good or bad. It's also highly subjective, i. e. why some people prefer well-done over medium, rare or blue steaks.

But while this is all true, there are subtleties pertaining to textural integrity that can greatly influence the customer experience, sometimes even without their knowing. This varies according to food type. For solid foods, could be about the sensory experience associated with fracture and breaking.

You may also hear the term mouthfeel, which is especially used for wine but also some foods. Mouthfeel also describes texture. While we perceive texture with our tongue, palates, and teeth, food scientists measure the texture of food by applying forces to it such as cutting, compressing, or shearing. They are determining the rheological aspects of the food.

(Adapted from *u 2 b. com*, *culinarylore. com*)

A2. Words and Expressions

Vocabulary

1. spicy /'spaɪsi / *adj*. 辣的
2. gingery /'dʒɪndʒəri / *adj*. 姜味的
3. acidic /ə'sɪdɪk / *adj*. 酸的
4. citrusy /'sɪtrəsi/ *adj*. 柠檬味的，橘味的
5. tangy /'tæŋi/ *adj*. 刺激的，浓烈的

Regular Food Taste	常规味觉
hot / spicy / peppery	辣的
garlicy	蒜味的，蒜香的
gingery	姜味的
creamy	奶油味的
buttery	黄油味的
fruity	水果味的
fresh	新鲜的
sour / acidic	酸的
citrusy / lemony	柠檬味的，橘味的
tangy	柠檬般的刺激味，浓烈的
fishy	鱼味的，有鱼腥味的
sweet	甜的
salty	咸的
tingly-numbing / tongue-numbing	麻的
mouth-burning	火烧般的（如芥末、辣椒等引起）
mellow	香醇的，浓厚的
mature	成熟的
fragrant / aromatic	香的（泛指令人愉悦的香味）
smokey	烟熏味的
earthy	农家味的，接近食材原味的
light / bland / plain / flat	不腻的，清淡的，味淡的
intense	味重的，强烈的
strong	强烈的，味浓的，酒精浓度高的

Vocabulary

1. greasy /ˈgriːsi/ *adj*. 油腻的
2. astringent /əˈstrɪndʒənt / *adj*. 涩的
3. stale /steɪl/ *adj*. 不新鲜的
4. moldy /ˈmoʊldi / *adj*. 霉味的，发霉的
5. rancid /ˈrænsɪd/ *adj*. 变味的，发臭的

Unpleasant Food Taste	不愉悦的味觉
oily	多油的
greasy	油腻的
fatty	多脂的
stale	不新鲜的(久置导致,尤指糕点)
moldy	霉味的
astringent / dry	涩的(常见于酒类引致的涩)
puckery	涩的(由其他味觉引起,如苦味)
bitter	苦的
gamey	野外动物或鸟类身上自带的味(如膻味)
nauseous / disgusting	恶心的
odious / stinky	发臭的
rancid	变味的,发臭的(通常是油或脂肪不新鲜导致的)
pungent	辛辣的,刺激的

Vocabulary

1. crispy /ˈkrɪspi/ *adj*. 薄脆的
2. crunchy /ˈkrʌntʃi/ *adj*. 硬脆的
3. succulent /ˈsʌkjələnt/ *adj*. 多汁的
4. al dente /ˌæl ˈdenteɪ/ *adj*. 劲道的
5. slimy /ˈslaɪmi/ *adj*. 丝滑的
6. glutinous /ˈɡluːtənəs/ *adj*. 黏的
7. gooey /ˈɡuːi/ *adj*. 软黏的,黏糊的
8. jiggly /ˈdʒɪɡli/ *adj*. Q 弹的,摇晃的

Food Texture	口感
crispy	鲜脆的,酥脆的(薄脆)
crunchy	松脆的,爽脆的(硬脆)
flaky / crumbly	脆酥的,易碎的,易脱落的
juicy / succulent	多汁的

watery	水分充足的
soft	软的
moist	松软,湿软味的
hard	硬的
tender	软嫩的
tough	老的,嚼不烂的
chewy	有嚼劲的
al dente	劲道的(常见于面类)
slimy / silky / smooth	丝滑的
sticky / tacky / glutinous	黏的,黏牙的
mushy / pulpy	软而稠的,糊状的
gooey	软而黏的,黏黏糊糊的
gritty / sandy	沙砾般的
starchy	富含淀粉的
fizzy / gassy	带气(二氧化碳)的
icy	结冰的,带冰的
fluffy	松软的,蓬松的
jiggly	Q 弹的
soggy	受潮的
thick	稠的
thin	稀的

A3. Situational Conversations

Conversation 1 Inviting a Foreign Friend for Dinner

L: Liu T: Tim

L: It's very nice of you to invite me.

T: I'm very glad you could come, Mr. Liu. Will you take a seat at the head of the table? It's an informal dinner, please don't **stand on ceremony**.... Mr. Liu, would you like to have some chicken?

L: Thank you. This is my first time to come to a Chinese restaurant. Could you tell me the different features of Chinese food?

T: Generally speaking, Cantonese food is a bit light; Shanghai food is rather oily; and

Hunan dishes are very spicy, having a strong and hot taste.

L: Chinese dishes are **exquisitely prepared**, delicious, and very palatable. They are very good in color, flavor, and taste.

T: Mr. Liu, would you care for another helping?

L: No more, thank you. I'm quite full.

T: Did you enjoy the meal?

L: It's the most delicious dinner I've had for a long time. It's such a rich dinner.

T: I'm so glad you like it.

L: Thank you very much for your **hospitality**.

(Adapted from *kekenet. com*)

> ☞ **Notes**
>
> - **stand on ceremony:** It means to behave in a formal way.
> - **exquisitely prepared:** It refers to food that is prepared in a very delicate way before being cooked.
> - **hospitality:** It refers to the kindness in welcoming guests or strangers.

Conversation 2 Healthy Diet

A healthy diet is a diet that helps to maintain or improve overall health. A healthy diet provides the body with essential nutrition: fluid, macronutrients, micronutrients, and adequate calories. Lily and Jessica are talking about healthy food.

L: Lily J: Jessica

L: Jessica, you're **in the pink**!

J: Thank you. I've dumped the junk food and now I like to eat some healthy food.

L: Well, I still like to eat crispy chips and I am gaining weight these days.

J: If you want to be healthy, first you need to change your diet. It is time for you to say goodbye to fatty food. Green diet is good for you.

L: I know. but I can't help having it.

J: Control yourself! Junk food has too much salt, sugar and fat. It's harmful for you.

L: Maybe I shouldn't **indulge** myself too much.

J: Yes, chips have too much oil. You'd better have more fruit vegetables and drink more water.

L: Anything else?

J: Try some Chinese food. Those Chinese light meals are also delicious.

L: Light meals are also good for health?

J: Of course. People are advised to eat less salt and sugar.

L: I'll have a try.

(Adapted from *en 8848 .com.cn*)

☞**Notes**

- **in the pink**: In perfect condition, especially of health.
  What's the origin of the phrase "in the pink?" The general usage of this phrase has altered somewhat since it first entered the language. We now usually see it with the specific meaning of "the pink of condition," that is, in the best possible health. It is tempting but, as it turns out, misguided, to assume an association between "the pink of condition" and the healthily glowing pink cheeks of new-born babies or energetic sportsmen / sportswomen and the like.
  (Retrieved from *quora.com*)
- **indulge**: It means allowing yourself to have or do something that you enjoy.

Conversation 3 It Smells Tasty

L: Linda G: Gary

L: All the food smells tasty today and **makes my mouth water.**

G: Let's line up here. This line seems a little shorter.

L: What's on the menu today?

G: Fish, beef, pork, chicken, vegetables and beancurd. For staple food we have rice, steamed bread, stuffed buns and noodles.

L: Oh, we're lucky today, aren't we?

G: I'd rather take stewed cabbage with beef.

L: I think I'll take fried fish, because fish is one of my favorites.

G: That's good, we can share what we have. Here we are. You go ahead.

L: (They get everything ready) Here is a free table. Let's sit down. Help yourself to some fish please. Isn't it delicious and **appetizing**?

G: I'm sorry I don't like it. It's a little too salty.

L: I see. You people from south prefer sweet, don't you?

G: Yes, I like the fish cooked in sweet and sour sauce best. Try some beef, it is pretty tender and juicy.

L: Thank you. I'm through with one steamed bread and I'd like **a second helping**.

G: Your appetite is good.

L: I'm always feeling hungry.

(Adapted from *kekenet. com*)

> ☞ **Notes**
>
> - **make one's mouth water**: To allow saliva (liquid in the mouth) to flow out of your mouth, it can also be described as "mouthwatering" in adjective.
> - **appetizing**: It refers to something that smells or looks attractive and makes you feel hungry or thirsty, and it is always appealing to or stimulating the appetite especially in appearance or aroma.
> - **a second helping**: It refers to a second amount of food given to one person at one time.

A4. Picture Knowledge

Cooking Verbs

Pic. 5-1

A Glosssary of Egg Dishes

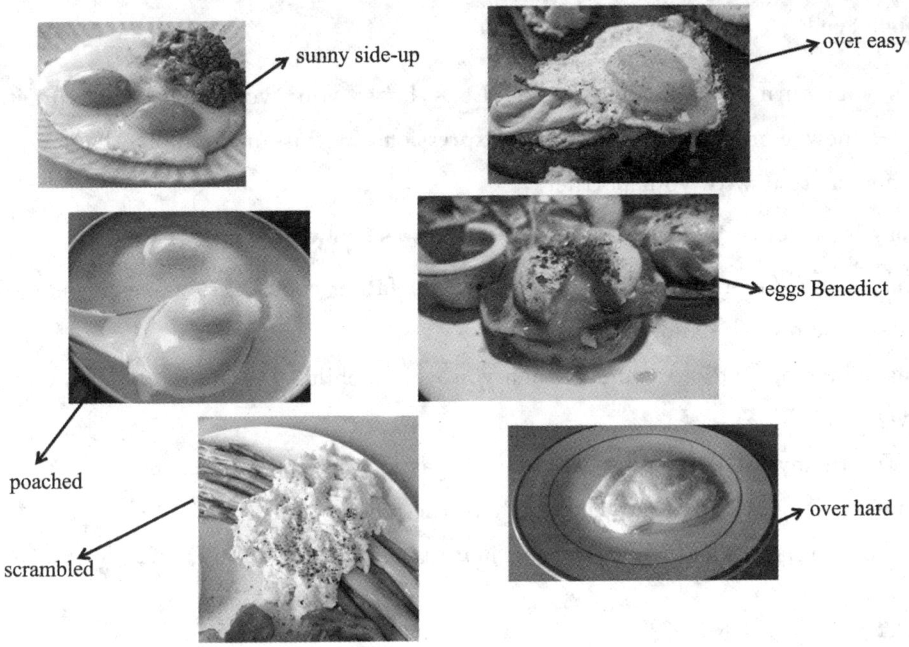

Pic. 5-2

Kitchen Utensils

Pic. 5-3

A5. Speaking Activities

Talk about Food

Now it's your turn to talk about food! Let's boost your vocabulary with practice. Choose 5-8 new words from **Words and Expressions** in this unit, apply them to your story, then share it with your partner.

Your story is suggested to cover two or three topics as below:

- What is your favorite food that your mother / father cooks? How does it taste? Try to describe its taste and texture.
- What kinds of food did you eat when you were a child? Do you eat the same things now?
- Are there any foods that you wouldn't eat as a child that you eat now?
- What kinds of food can you cook? Share the recipe.
- Would you like to learn how to cook more types of food? Why?

Discussion

Conduct a group discussion on your personal diet habit and see if you could agree on what is healthy diet.

The following facts are for your reference:

Two-thirds of American women and half of American men want to lose weight.

Obesity now rivals smoking as a major cause of death.

More than half of Americans are overweight.

30 percent of Americans are clinically obese.

Greater numbers of children are suffering from type 2 diabetes — which used to be called "adult-onset" diabetes — a disease associated with diet and lifestyle.

$40 billion per year is being spent, with very poor results, on the diet industry.

90 percent of dieters gain back everything they have lost within a year.

(Adapted from *pbs. org*)

Retelling

Read the passage about Chinese dumpling and retell how to make it with details.

A Journey to the Jiaozi

Jiaozi, or what we in English call dumplings, are one of the quintessential foods eaten during Spring Festival and it's common for all the family to help in the preparations.

Today I'm cooking alongside my colleague Christy Lee who informs me we're making the pork and cabbage variety. First, we add wheat flour into a bowl, with a bit of water to make a thick dough that we then knead on a board. As Christy Lee explains, from here things start to get a bit more meaty, and in Chinese custom, heavy handed chopping was considered a good way to scare off bad spirits. Then it's time to add some spring onion, ginger and Chinese cabbage and after all the fun of chopping then mix it all together adding a bit of soy sauce, salt and spice. As you can see it got a little messy. So reaching for the blob of dough makes a lifesaver and then separate that into two pieces, which are then further rolled and small pellets are snapped off about an inch in size.

With these you then flatten firmly between both hands and then take a rolling pin holding the dough in the center lightly flatten just the outer edges — turning clockwise in quarter turns. Once you have your dumpling pillows ready it's time to pack in your filling and then gently squeeze the edges to create a picturesque crimped seal. As with many things it looks easy until you try doing it yourself. With the pot boiling place your jiaozi lovingly in one by one and once you've got about 15 in give them a soft stir using the back of a ladle making sure they don't stick to the pot or bust their load. And in a few minutes there you have it. The broth in the pot is also said to aid in digestion.

(Adapted from *chinadaily. com. cn*)

Interpretation

Interpret the following paragraphs into English with what you have learned in Part A.

Paragraph 1

个人而言，我的口味偏淡。我最喜欢的食物是粤式点心。同时，我也很喜欢四川菜，但是吃不了太辣的菜，因为它会导致我的肠胃有火烧的感觉，甚至会引起胃痛和消化不良等问题。此外，我还喜欢酸味，所以我总是在食物里面放一点醋，喝可乐的时候喜欢加点柠檬汁来提味。

Paragraph 2

一天之计在于晨，一天的营养也在于早餐。我的早餐种类繁多且营养丰富。我母亲每天都会准备好豆浆或者牛奶、馒头、煎蛋（两面煎-全熟）、蔬菜沙拉等。饭后，我还会喝一杯现磨咖啡，我个人喜欢拿铁，它是我每天的精神源泉，让我活力四射、注意力高度集中。

Paragraph 3

我比较喜欢两道菜：酸辣土豆丝和蒜香牛肉。做好酸辣土豆丝最重要的一点是处理好土豆。先去皮，然后切成片，再切成丝，最后需要用清水浸泡，这样才能使土豆清脆。而做好蒜香牛肉需要选用鲜嫩的牛肉和新鲜的大蒜，整个爆炒过程必须使用大火。一道成功的蒜香牛肉往往入口多汁而不肥腻，肉质劲道有嚼劲。

Paragraph 4

西式快餐的优缺点均十分明显。它的主要缺点在于热量过高，不够健康。优点在于，食物酥脆可口、快速做成且便于携带。当然，吃太多油炸食物会让人觉得油腻。个人而言，我最喜欢辛辣味的汉堡及美式咖啡，每天来一杯黑咖总是让我能量满满。此外，免费续杯让我觉得性价比很高。

A6. Extension

Synonym Discrimination

Can you figure out the differences among the words below?

Group 1: light / bland / insipid / plain / dull / tasteless / flavorless
Group 2: heavy / intense / thick / strong / dense

Extensive Reading

Why Chinese Cooking Became So Popular in the West

Even though attitudes had begun to change, the West still had a stereotypical view of Chinese food with many just assuming it was all sweet and sour. It took time and alteration of traditional dishes for it to truly pick up traction.

George Charles

Chinese food has become a staple in the world, with many giving it top billing when it comes to a favourite cuisine type; yet surprisingly this hasn't always been the case. It's hard now to imagine a world without delicious Chinese food being readily available, be it through takeaway deliveries, fine dining restaurants or home cooked experiments. Similarly, many Britons would now find it impossible to remember a time when authentic sauces weren't readily available in all supermarkets, yet there was a time where all this delicious food choice was completely alien.

It's thought that the first Chinese immigrants came to the shores of the UK in the early

19th century, which is around the time the first ever Chinese restaurant opened (1908). This establishment was very creatively called "The Chinese Restaurant" and was located in Piccadilly Circus, London. Although this was a massive breakthrough for the cuisine, it didn't pick up popularity for years.

Back in the 1950s the idea of Chinese food in the UK and America was simplistic; tinned Chinese curries, processed foods and confused flavours, like Chinese food on pizza. Take out venues were few and far between and other cuisines with less experimental flavours were favoured by Western palates.

It wasn't until the 60s and 70s that Chinese food began getting the recognition it deserved. More citizens began arriving on Western soil from Hong Kong and Chinatown development started in the 70s, when chefs began talking about exotic flavours. One pivotal figure during this period was Kenneth Lo, who is credited as being an ambassador of Chinese cuisine to the West. He wrote more than 30 books on Chinese cooking from the 1950s to the 1990s, with over one million copies sold in Britain. One of his most popular books, simply titles "Chinese Food" was released in the 1970s, a time which was significant for the growth in interest of Chinese cuisine.

Lo also opened a cooking school in London during the 1980s, which was hailed as Europe's first Chinese cooking school. Alongside this, people began opening up to the idea of varied flavours but dishes had to make the most of ingredients available in the West. Chinese chefs began to adapt dishes to use readily available ingredients and also appeal more to western palates. This ended up creating dishes that a Western audience perceives as Chinese but you wouldn't even find in China. For example, Chop Suey is used to be one of the most popular dishes found in the West but you wouldn't be able to find this dish with ease in China. Same goes for Egg Foo Young and even the beloved fortune cookies.

Even though attitudes had begun to change, the West still had a stereotypical view of Chinese food with many just assuming it was all sweet and sour. It took time and alteration of traditional dishes for it to truly pick up traction. Education on the region and the foods that originated here, conducted by high profile chefs, such as Ken Hom, Andrew Wong and Ching He-Huang, and new celebrity chefs of Chinese origin helped change the public's opinion on the seemingly exotic dishes.

More frequent travel of British to the Far East for business or leisure has exposed consumers to more varieties and both authentic and modern Chinese flavours.

The West's perception of Chinese food has gone from merely eating a Chinese takeaway dish each week to consumers experimenting themselves by using Oriental flavours in their kitchens. The highest quality food has become sought after by modern day diners, meaning home cooked meals and even those purchased at fine dining establishments are now often preferred over takeaways. No longer do those living in the west fear complex, unfamiliar and unaccustomed flavours, instead they embrace the contrast and try to incorporate them into their diet.

There are healthier options available for those ordering a Chinese to their house which has helped these establishments maintain their popularity in a society that has started caring more about what it is they put in their bodies. Steaming is one of the healthiest and most common cooking methods found in Chinese cuisine. Many chefs choose to steam their ingredients, like tofu, to retain the health benefits of the food without compromising on flavour. And there are plenty of cooking methods under the Chinese umbrella yet to be explored by the West.

With better and in-depth understanding of what Chinese cooking and diet offer will put this healthy culinary style into perspective.

The modern world is now well wired; the media has generated curiosity of cross cultural understanding and food is obviously one of the most used mediums to communicate.

Chinese food has continuously adapted to the tastes of the west which has led to a steady increase in its popularity; it shows no signs of stopping and it never will.

(Adapted from *HuffPost*)

Part B Food Culture and Communication

B1. Introduction

Differences Between Eastern and Western Eating Habits

Mabel Kwong

There are different ways of dining all around the world. Different cultures, especially eastern and western cultures, have different ways of eating, cooking and serving food. Evidently there were noticeably different eating habits and food preferences between each other's cultures.

Utensils

Eating with fork and spoon is the norm in Western cultures, and so is eating with a knife when a good chunk of meat is served. There can be a unique utensil for each course of a meal, such as in French dining. While many of Asian background eat with fork and spoons, many also eat with chopsticks or eating with just their hands. For instance, it's common for Muslims to eat with their right hand and this is in line with their faith. For some Indians it's a mark of respect (especially to the host) to physically touch the food one is eating — joining all fingers together and picking up food to eat, in a way creating a spiritual connection with what one is eating.

Cooking techniques

Steaming, boiling and stir frying are popular Chinese cooking methods. Popular and staple Chinese dishes include soup and pan-fried dumplings, steamed veggies with oyster sauce and simmered bone broths. In contrast many popular Western dishes in Australia tend to be on the fried or baked side: fried chicken, pizza, fish and chips, meat pies and lamb roast. Notably in Asian culture dishes are more or less served warm or hot and rarely raw and cold (sushi would be the popular exception). On the other hand, salads, yoghurts and cheeses are popular "cold" gastronomic choices among many Westerners.

Table and seating configuration

Dining at round tables is common in Asian cultures and encourages inclusivity no matter where one sits. Dining at a round table, everyone can see each other — it encourages everyone to chat and connect with each other (one can see everyone at the table face to face), it's convenient to pass food around on a Lazy Susan in the middle of the table. Also, the eldest or most senior person usually takes the seat facing the entrance, symbolic of hierarchical respect. Eating at rectangular tables is more common in

Western cultures. One might not get the chance to chat with every single person when seated at this kind of table but might be highly encouraged to make small chat with the person beside or right in front of them.

Sharing vs. individual dishes

In Chinese culture most dishes are designed to be shared over rice or noodles, and rice and noodles are supposed to be eaten along with other dishes. Not to say there aren't individual dishes in Chinese culture — for example duck noodles and Hainanese chicken rice are dishes that ones would have to all themselves. But many if not most Chinese dishes are really meant to be shared. Individual dishes are more common in Western cultures and it's not surprising for someone to order one dish and have it all to themselves. On the plus side, when everyone orders a dish for themselves, it can be easier when it's time to pay the bill: everyone eats their own share, fair and square pays for their own dish, no need to fight over the bill.

Balance and variety

There is usually a starter / entrée, main and dessert when it comes to having many a Western meal. Sometimes this includes a salad and cheese course. While multicourse meals are also part of Asian dining, balance is key here: There is usually a soup, a base of rice or noodles and a vegetable and meat dish served. With Asian cuisine, there is a focus on optimising meals for digestion — aligning with the concept of Yin and Yang — rather than stuffing oneself and feeling satiated and even more satiated.

Drinks

Having an alcoholic beverage for lunch or dinner is pretty common in Australia. Beer is always on the drink menu when it comes to eating at many Asian restaurants here in Melbourne. Warm tea is usually the first drink to be offered when dining Chinese and in many Chinese eateries. Soy bean milk, milk tea and sugarcane juice are also drinks many Chinese like to order with their meals.

Flavors

Many Asian dishes are bold and aromatic in flavor. It's the ingredients used that bring out these flavors, ingredients such as vinegar, five spice powder, cooking wine, hoisin sauce and soy sauce. Ginger and garlic are also staple ingredients in many Chinese dishes, and there's usually the option of added chili too. In western cuisine, chili isn't served with every meal. Processed sauces seemed to be served more with Western food. Tomato sauce, mustard, mayonnaise, barbecue sauce are some popular sauces one finds with American, European and Australian cuisine.

Dessert

Fruit is a popular dessert option in Asian cuisine. Some popular Asian desserts include sweet sticky rice pudding, peanut soup, egg tarts and lotus seed paste balls. On the other hand, ice-cream is always a popular dessert option at the end of a Western meal, and so is the choice of brownie and cake.

(Adapted from *mabelkwong.com*)

B2. Words and Expressions

Vocabulary

1. reserve /rɪˈzɜːrv/ *v.* 预定
2. booth /buːθ/ *n.* 卡座
3. booster /ˈbuːstər/ *n.* 帮助(改善、激励)……的事物
4. specialty /ˈspeʃəlti/ *n.* 特色菜,招牌菜
5. combo /ˈkɑːmboʊ/ *n.* 不同食物的合餐、大杂烩,套餐
6. appetizer /ˈæpɪtaɪzər/ *n.* 开胃菜,开胃饮料
7. salad /ˈsæləd/ *n.* 沙拉
8. dessert /dɪˈzɜːrt/ *n.* 甜品

Order Food	**点餐**
reserve a table	预定餐桌
window seat	靠窗的座位,窗座
corner table	边角桌子
corner seat	边角座位
a table with street / sea view	带街(海)景的餐桌
a table for two, please	请安排一张双人桌
booth	卡座
high chair	幼儿高脚椅
booster seat	儿童加高座
menu, please	请给我菜单
order, please	点菜
specialty	特色菜,招牌菜
special meals	特餐
combo	不同食物的合餐、大杂烩,套餐
individual serving	分餐制
serving chopsticks	公筷
serving spoon	公勺

Serving Order	上菜顺序
starter / appetizer	头盘，开胃菜
soup	汤
vice dishes (fish / egg / bread)	副餐
salad	沙拉
main course	主菜
side dishes / sides (vegetable)	配菜，附加菜
dessert	甜品
drink (coffee / beverage)	饮品

Vocabulary

1. savory /ˈseɪvəri/ *adj.* 美味的，可口的
2. palatable /ˈpælətəbl/ *adj.* 美味的，可口的
3. lousy /ˈlaʊzi/ *adj.* 糟糕的，恶劣的
4. Dutch /dʌtʃ/ *adj.* 荷兰的，荷兰人的，荷兰语的
5. split /splɪt/ *v.* 分担，分摊
6. leftover /ˈleftoʊvər/ *n.* 剩饭，剩菜
7. doggie /ˈdɒgi/ *n.* 狗狗（儿语）
8. toothpick /ˈtuːθpɪk/ *n.* 牙签
9. disposable /dɪˈspoʊzəbl/ *adj.* 一次性的，用完即丢弃的

Comment Food	评价食物
yummy / tasty / savory / flavorful / palatable / toothsome	美味的，可口的
finger licking	舔指般美味
delicious / delish (inf.)	非常美味的
yucky	难吃的
lousy	糟糕的
awful	可怕的
taste like a disaster	难吃（灾难般的，比喻）
taste like a cardboard	味如嚼蜡

Pay the Check / Bill	付费
check / bill, please	请给我账单
pay separately / let's go Dutch /	各付各的，平摊费用

go fifty-fifty / split the bill / go halves	
it is on me / my treat	请客
be my guest	请客
foot the bill	付账
keep the change	不用找零
leave a tip	留小费

Pack up Food	**打包**
for here, or to go?	在这吃,还是带走?
leftover	剩饭,剩菜
doggie bag	剩菜袋,打包袋
to-go box / food box	打包盒
toothpick	牙签
disposable gloves / chopsticks / spoon	一次性手套/筷子/勺子

B3. Situational Conversations

Conversation 1 Keep Modest at a Chinese Dinner

A: Alan K: Kate

A: The last thing to be ignored at a Chinese dinner table is to **keep modest**.

K: Does that suggest diners avoid speaking much? The same is true in the West.

A: No, absolutely not! On the contrary, you'll be considered **a well-connected**, sociable **man**, if you keep involved in the conversation all the time. But always pay attention to what you say. If the table has a senior guest, **say something** as **upbeat** and cheerful as possible. Or maybe, you may give the floor to him and keep listening as if very interested.

K: You mean, **keeping a low profile** in the presence of the old? That goes in like with Confucius' preaching, right?

A: Correct. Show respect for the older people. Conventionally, before the meal starts, the younger members are supposed to address each one of the elderly members of the table one by one. Others are kept in waiting until the most venerable guest proclaims the beginning of the meal and takes the first bite. **Toasts** also go to these men first before people can toast to each other.

K: Any other rules to observe in order to keep modest?

A: Yes, plenty of them. Don't eat fast! People usually keep their dining pace accorded with others. And all the dishes should not be eaten up completely.

K: Is it because that would give the host the impression that the food was insufficient?

A: Hah, I'm afraid it's simply because no one wishes to be too noticeable by finishing off the plate.

(Adapted from *kekenet.com*)

☞**Notes**

- **keep modest**: It is used to describe one who is not usually talking about or making obvious one's own abilities and achievements, and it has similar meaning like **keep humble.**
- **a well-connected man**: It refers to a man having friends or family members who are important or powerful people.
- **say something upbeat**: It means to say something full of hope, happiness, and good feelings.
- **keep a low profile**: It means to avoid attracting attention to oneself, and shapes a contrast of the expression — **keep a high profile.**
- **a toast**: It is an expression of good wishes or respect for someone that involves holding up and then drinking from a glass of alcohol, especially wine, after a short speech.

Conversation 2 Select a Restaurant

J: John K: Kate

J: Do you want to go out for dinner tonight?

K: Sure. Have you got anywhere in mind?

J: I'm starving, so maybe we could go somewhere with large portions.

K: That Italian restaurant in the city center always has large portions. Do you want to go there?

J: I'm not really in the mood for Italian, actually. I was thinking of something a bit spicy.

K: If you want spicy food, then I'd recommend going to a Thai, Indian or Chinese restaurant. How about that Chinese buffet on Cowley Road?

J: I really like that restaurant; you get a lot for your money there. But, they've **westernized** their **food**, so it's not actually that spicy.

K: You're right. Most of their dishes have sweet sauces. We could try that Indian restaurant just down the road from us.

J: The Taj? They're a bit expensive, but they do serve large portions of very hot food.

K: The Taj it is then.

J: Shall we bring our own bottle of wine to save some money?

K: They'll still charge us a **corkage fee.**

J: That's right. It'll probably work out to be about the same then anyway.

K: Don't worry about money. I'll treat you tonight.

J: Are you sure? We could go Dutch.

K: No, I'll pay. It's my turn anyway. You paid last time.

J: I won't argue with that! Let's go!

(Adapted from *kekenet.com*)

☞**Notes**

- **westernized food**: It refers to the food having a culture like North America and western Europe. A large majority of westernized Chinese food is deep fried or soaked in sauce, while deep frying is rarely practiced in China. Most authentic Chinese dishes are stewed, braised, baked, steamed or boiled and utilize spices rather than sauces and salt.

  (Adapted from *escoffieronline.com*)

- **corkage fee**: A corkage fee is the price charged to guests who choose to bring their own bottle of wine to a restaurant. Corkage fees usually exist at restaurants that already serve wine. The practice of allowing guests to bring their own wine is considered a courtesy to guests.

  Occasionally, a bar or restaurant might charge a corkage fee for providing their own wine as a means of raising their bottom line or covering their wine service costs.

  In most restaurants, corkage fees are per bottle. Corkage fees might also be per table or per person (known as per glass or per "stem").

  If bringing in your own bottle, some restaurants waive the corkage fee if you also purchase a bottle of their wine.

  (Adapted from *webstaurantstore.com*)

Conversation 3 Order Food

W: Waiter P: Paul J: Jane

W: Hello, I will be your waitress today. Can I get you both any drinks?
P: Yes. I would like an iced coffee, please.
J: And I will have the same please.
W: OK, two iced coffees, here you are. Are you now ready to order, or would you like a few more minutes?
P: I think we are ready to order. I will have the chicken soup to start, and the steak with fries and the mixed vegetables.
W: How do you want the steak cooked rare, medium, or well done?
P: I would like it well done, please.
J: I do not want a starter. I would like to have the fried chicken with fries and a side

salad please.

W: Your meals will be here shortly.

W: Here are your meals. If you need anything else just ask. Have a nice meal.

(Adapted from *easypacelearning.com*)

☞**Notes**

- **What is doneness of meat?**

  Doneness is a gauge of how thoroughly cooked a cut of meat is based on its color, juiciness, and internal temperature when cooked. The gradations of cooking are most often used in reference to beef but are also applicable to lamb, pork, poultry, veal, and seafood.

  (Retrieved from *Wikipedia.com*)

- **What are the differences and degrees of steak doneness?**

  Rare: very red

  Medium rare: warm, red center

  Medium: pink center

  Medium well: slightly pink center

  Well: cooked throughout, no pink

B4. Picture Knowledge

Formal Table Setting

Pic. 5-4

Different Types of Containers

Pic. 5-5

Different Types of Bread

Pic. 5-6

B5. Speaking Activities

Role Play

One student roleplays the restaurant patron while another is the server. In the role play, you should put the food language learned in this unit into practice.

You may refer to the expressions below but don't confine yourself to them.

Suggested Expressions:

- **Asking about the menu:**
  What's ... exactly?
  What do you recommend?
  Is this served with ... (salad)?
  Does this have any ... (seafood) in it?
  Could I have it without ... ?
  I don't like...
- **Dealing with problems:**
  For customer:
  Excuse me, but I didn't order this.
  I'm sorry, but this is cold.
  Can I change my order please?
  For waiter:
  I'm so sorry about that....
  Let me take it back for you. (take it back=return it to the kitchen)
  Let me change it for you.

Menu Design

Work in pairs to design a menu. Your menu should cover the name of your restaurant, the name of each dish as well as its ingredients. Then introduce your menu to the class. You may refer to the expressions below but don't confine yourself to them.

- **Include the following items:**
  a. appetizers
  b. soup(s) of the day
  c. salads and / or salad bar
  d. entrees / main dishes
  e. side orders (which may include breads)
  f. beverages (non-alcoholic, please!)
  g. desserts

- **Earn bonus points by including the following:**
  a. Chef's Specials
  b. Special(s) of the Day
  c. Early Bird Specials
  d. Dieter's / Lo-Cal Specials
  e. Vegetarian Specials

(Adapted from *readwritethink.org*)

Discussion

Conduct a pair discussion and summarize your viewpoints. Imagine that you are a college student living off campus, you have to cook on your own. As for homemade food and store-bought food, which do you prefer? State the reasons.

Interpretation

Interpret the following paragraphs into English with what you have learned in Part B.

Paragraph 1

在学校,我一般都会选择去食堂吃饭。我认为食堂的食物比较干净,卫生有保障。尽管很多人说食堂的菜缺少油水,口味过于大众化,没什么招牌菜,但我可以接受。我不喜欢订外卖,因为订外卖需要大量的打包盒、打包袋和一次性餐具。我认为这是浪费资源,而且会对环境产生不好的影响。我更喜欢绿色且经济的生活,所以去食堂吃饭对我来说是最好的选择。

Paragraph 2

上周六,我和好友一起去吃了牛排。牛排是这家店的特色菜,进门前我就闻到了食物的香气。我们点了七分熟的牛排和两面煎的鸡蛋,还要了意大利面及土豆泥。牛排尝起来多汁且鲜嫩,但是鸡蛋煎得有点硬了,意大利面也过于劲道。不过那里的卡布奇诺最受欢迎,不仅很香,还可免费续杯,所以我喝了很多。饭后,我们都争着请客,最后只好采取AA制。

Paragraph 3

在海外留学的时候,我特别喜欢去唐人街吃饭。每次去之前都会预定好一张靠窗的餐桌,可以看看街景,欣赏熙熙攘攘的人们,品尝家乡菜,就像回到了祖国,以此缓解我的思乡之苦。我经常带着各国好友一块去品尝中国美食,向他们介绍我们博大精深的饮食文化。当然,入乡随俗,我们会十分注意饮食卫生,一般采用分餐制并使用公筷。

B6. Extension

Synonym Discrimination

Can you figure out the differences among the words below?

Group 1: trim / peel / chop / dice / slice / shred / grate / mince / grind / smash / scale / debone / squeeze / crush
Group 2: pinch / whip / steam / sauté / fry / roll out / poke / rip / tear / rub / tap / press / flip / crack / crumple / pry / squash / grate / stir / grill
Group 3: braise / stew / simmer

Extensive Reading

Passage One

Calculate a Tip Without Pen and Paper or a Calculator

Deb Russell

It is customary to leave a tip for many services that are supplied by people like waiters and waitresses, taxi drivers, hotel maids, moving company staff and hair salon staff to name a few. The rule of thumb amount is 15%, although there are varying thoughts as to the amount that would be appropriate for exceptional service (usually 20%) and poor service (10% or less). Some people frown on giving no tip, as in many instances the server is not the reason for the service issue; traffic snarls and kitchen issues can be the problems and these people rely on tips to supplement their minimum wage.

So now that we have some ideas as to the etiquette involved, let's look at some simple math ideas to make the calculation simple but effective.

Easy way to calculate a 15% tip

Rule of thumb — standard service — 15%. The most commonly used shortcut to 15% is to find 10% and then add a half. This is an easy calculation, since all you need to do to find 10% is move the decimal point one space to the left (make the number smaller).

Consider a bill for 47.31. First impressions show us 10% is 4.70 and a half of this amount is 2.35, so a tip of 7.00 is reasonable. This is a simplification as we can do the exact math — 4.70 add 2.35 is 7.05 — but we are looking for an easy method, not an exacting science. Another sound strategy is to work from the highest place value, in other words, if the bill is in the 50s then the tip should be in the 7.50 range. If the bill is 124.00, the logic follows that 12 add 6 = 18 so a total of 124 add 18 or 142 is reasonable.

Calculating a tip based on sales tax

Another very sound strategy is to work from the sales tax. Look at your sales tax rates and devise a strategy based on the amount. In New York city, the tax on a meal is 8.75% so you can just double the amount of tax and your service provider is happy.

There are also some fun and unique answers to the question of how to do the math without straining yourself. Consider the following examples that people have provided: great service — bill times 10%, then doubled; less than great service — bill times 10%.

- For a bill under $50:
  Great service — bill times 10% then doubled — it will be over 15% and the appreciation should be noticed.
  Good service — somewhere in between great and less than good. Add a little to less than good and you will be safe.
  Less than good service — bill times 10%— the message will be conveyed but you are smart enough to realize that it may not be their fault alone.
- For a bill over $50:
  Make sure you start your calculations based on the pretax amount of your bill.
  Great service — 10% of the bill — doubled — round down.
  Less than great — 10% round down.

(Adapted from *thoughtco.com*)

Passage Two

What Does RSVP Mean on an Invitation?

Donna Pilato

The term "RSVP" comes from the French expression *répondez s'il vous plaît*, meaning "please respond." If RSVP is written on an invitation, it means the host has requested that the guest respond to say if they plan to attend the party.

RSVP vs. regrets only

If the RSVP says, "regrets only," you only need to respond if you are unable to attend. If you don't respond, the host will expect you to be there. Be sure to use the requested method to respond if you can't attend. It's best not to respond if you will attend, as a response may be confusing to the host. Use other methods to express your enthusiasm about attending the event.

How to RSVP

Invitations requiring an RSVP will have instructions how to respond. A formal invitation, such as a wedding invitation, will have an enclosed response card that you can return in its provided envelope. Informal invitations, on the other hand, may have a telephone number, email address, texting address, or social media method to reply, with instructions. Electronic RSVP requests make it easy to respond by either email or links to a site with buttons to accept or decline.

The RSVP should make it clear who is invited. Couples are often named together, sometimes followed by "and family," which would include your minor children. It may indicate you are able to bring a guest, often called a "Plus One." If you don't see any indication that the invitation allows you to bring a guest, you should assume it is only for you and anyone else explicitly named.

There may be a blank to write in a number of guests. Check further on the invitation to see what the limits are for a number of guests. If you are considering more than one or two, contact the host to ensure the event can handle the number you are proposing to bring.

When to RSVP

RSVP requests often include a deadline for response, as the host is finalizing numbers for the caterer, event site, favors, and other event details. It's best to respond as soon as possible rather than delaying. The host then may be able to offer invitations to other people who didn't make the first cut for invitations or accommodates extra guests of other invitees.

If you want to attend but are unable to give a definite response before the deadline, it's best to decline. You can contact the host with your regrets and explain what is keeping you from being able to know you can attend. Ask if there is any flexibility but understand if there isn't. The earlier you make this call, the better, rather than waiting until the host has followed up with requests to return the outstanding RSVPs.

Canceling or changing an RSVP

It is bad form to cancel an RSVP, with exceptions including illness or a death in your family. The host will already have made plans based on your attendance. The time to decline is when you make the RSVP, considering all the factors as to your scheduling, finances, and other opportunities. If you declined the RSVP but discover you can attend the event, contact the host to see if it is possible.

Why it's inconsiderate not to RSVP

Many people don't RSVP because they don't want to disappoint the host. This attempt to spare their feelings usually causes more trouble than a simple no. An incomplete list of respondents can cause numerous problems for a host, including difficulty in planning food quantities, issues relating to minimum guarantees with catering halls, uncertainty over the number of party favors, and difficulties in planning appropriate seating, among other things.

Sometimes people don't send an RSVP by the requested time because they are unsure if they will be able to attend and don't want to commit to an answer. If this is your situation, it's best to be honest with the host about your situation. The only way they can help make accommodations for you is if they know you need them.

(Adapted from *thespruce. com*)

Sources of Pictures

Pic. 5-1 Edited and processed by authors
Pic. 5-2 Edited and processed by authors
Pic. 5-3 Edited and processed by authors
Pic. 5-4 Retrieved from *johnlewis. scene 7 . com*
Pic. 5-5 Edited and processed by authors
Pic. 5-6 Edited and processed by authors

References

Aisyah Liliana. (2020). A Sensory Approach to Food. *U2b*. Retrieved from https://u2b.com/2020/01/09/taste-smell-texture-a-sensory-approach-to-customer-experience-food/on July 29th, 2020.

Journey to the Jiaozi: A Hearty, Healthy Spring Festival. *China Daily*. Retrieved from http://www. chinadaily. com. cn/video/2009-01/23/content_7713604. htm on July 29th, 2020.

Deb Russell. (2018). Calculate a Tip Without Pen and Paper or a Calculator. *Thoughtco*. Retrieved from https://www. thoughtco. com/how-to-mentally-calculate-tips-2312564 on July 29th, 2020.

Donna Pilato. (2020). What Does RSVP Mean on an Invitation?. *Thespruce*. Retrieved from https://www. thespruce. com/what-does-rsvp-mean-on-invitations-1196806 on July 29th, 2020.

EricT_Culinarylore. (2020). What is Food Texture?. *Culinarylore*. Retrieved from https://culinarylore. com/food-science:what-is-food-texture/on July 29th, 2020.

Graham Aubert. (2019). Healthy Diet, in the Pink. *Quora*. Retrieved from https://www. quora. com/Which-is-correct-in-the-pink-or-in-the-pink-of-health on July 29th, 2020.

Hannah Herrera. Select a Restaurant, Corkage Fee. *Webstaurantstore*. Retrieved from https://www. webstaurantstore. com/blog/2626/corkage-fee-guide. html#:~:text=The%20average%20corkage%20fee%20ranges%20from%20%2410%20to, least%

20expensive%20wine.%20Are%20Corkage%20Fees%20Per%20Bottle%3F on July 29th, 2020.

Mabel Kwong. (2018). 10 Differences Between Eastern and Western Eating Habits. *Mabelkwong*. Retrieved from https://mabelkwong.com/2018/06/21/10-differences-between-eastern-and-western-eating-habits/on July 29th, 2020.

Merryangle87. (2013). Healthy Diet. *En*8848. Retrieved from https://www.en8848.com.cn/kouyu/live/tdshdh/213046.html? p=2 on July 29th, 2020.

Miyo. (2014). At a Chinese Restaurant. *Kekenet*. Retrieved from http://talk.kekenet.com/show_2564 on July 29th, 2020.

Miyo. (2014). It Smells Tasty. *Kekenet*. Retrieved from http://talk.kekenet.com/show_2556 on July 29th, 2020.

Miyo. (2014). Situational Conversations: Keep Modest at a Chinese Dinner. *Kekenet*. Retrieved from http://talk.kekenet.com/show_2444 on July 29th, 2020.

Miyo. (2014). Situational Conversations: Select a Restaurant. *Kekenet*. Retrieved from http://talk.kekenet.com/show_2492 on July 29th, 2020.

Pat Grimmer. Diet Wars. *Pbs.org*. Retrieved from https://www.pbs.org/wgbh/pages/frontline/teach/diet/on July 29th, 2020.

George Charles. Why Chinese Cooking Became So Popular in the West. *HuffPost*. Retrieved from https://www.huffingtonpost.co.uk/george—charles/why—chinese—cooking—becam_b_17464058.html on July 29th, 2020.

Order Food. E*asypacelearning*. Retrieved from https://www.easypacelearning.com/all-lessons/english-lessons-level-3/1351-restaurant-conversation-arriving-and-ordering-food-conversation on July 29th, 2020.

Select a Restaurant, Westernized Food. *Escoffieronline*. Retrieved from https://www.escoffieronline.com/the-westernization-of-chinese-food/on July 29th, 2020.

Susan H. Smith. Menu Magic!. *Readwritethink.org*. Retrieved from http://www.readwritethink.org/files/resources/lesson_images/lesson842/VM0104Menu.pdf on July 29th, 2020.

Wikipedia, the free encyclopedia. (2020). Doneness. *Wikipedia*. Retrieved from https://en.wikipedia.org/wiki/Doneness on July 29th, 2020.